THE TEMPLARS' SECRET ISLAND

THE AUTHORS

Erling Haagensen lives and works on the island of Bornholm. He is a well-known documentary film maker in Denmark and has made several hundred television programmes. In 1992 he produced and directed for TV-2 Danmark a four-part series *The Secrets of the Knights Templar* which was written and presented by Henry Lincoln. This was later shown all over the world by the Discovery channel. *The Templars' Secret Island* is based on more than ten years of research and a shorter version of it was first published in Denmark in 1993. The present English version contains further research and is a close collaboration with Henry Lincoln.

Henry Lincoln began his career in the theatre and first wrote for television in the early 1960s. He encountered the Mystery of Rennes-le-Château in 1969, which was his first BBC documentary film.

In the three decades since, he has concentrated almost exclusively on writing historical documentary scripts and four books delving into the secrets of Rennes-le-Château. They include his most recent work *Key to the Sacred Pattern*, the bestselling *The Holy Blood and the Holy Grail* and *The Messianic Legacy* (co-authored with Richard Leigh and Michael Baigent).

Other books by Henry Lincoln

The Holy Blood and the Holy Grail
 co-authored with Michael Baigent and Richard Leigh

The Messianic Legacy
 co-authored with Michael Baigent and Richard Leigh

The Holy Place

The Key to the Sacred Pattern

THE TEMPLARS' SECRET ISLAND

The Knights, the Priest and the Treasure

BY ERLING HAAGENSEN AND HENRY LINCOLN

CASSELL&CO

A WINDRUSH PRESS BOOK

First published in the United Kingdom in 2000 by The Windrush Press.
This edition reprinted in association with Cassell & Co, 2002.

ISBN 1-84188-190-2

Designed by Mark-making Design Ltd
Printed and bound by The Cromwell Press, Trowbridge, Wiltshire

Cassell & Co.
Wellington House
125 Strand
London WC2R OBB

The Windrush Press
Windrush House
Adlestrop
Moreton-in-Marsh
Gloucestershire GL56 OYN
Telephone: 01608 658758
Fax: 01608 659345

For Hedda and J
who are sometimes
– like certain numbers –
irrational
but are, of course,
always
transcendental

CONTENTS

List of Illustrations   ix
Acknowledgements   xi

PART ONE: FACTS

1 BEGINNINGS   3
   The Pathways   4
   The Other World   7

2 THE ENIGMATIC ISLAND   9
   Bornholm's Churches   14
   Gothic Architecture   15
   The Magic of Number   18

3 SECRETS OF THE KNIGHTS TEMPLAR   23
   Beliefs and Hypotheses   25
   Jerusalem   27
   St Bernard of Clairvaux   29
   The Scandinavian Link   30
   Crusade   36

4 THE INVISIBLE PATTERN   41
   Extended Search   49
   Olsker   55

5 STAR PATTERNS   57
   Symbolism   59
   Christiansø   61
   The Five-Pointed Star   64

6 UNITS OF MEASURE   69
   The Metre, the Yard and the Pole   72
   The English Measure   73
   Grail Sidelight   77
   Earth Measure   80
   Symbolic Precision   82

PART TWO: BELIEFS

7	UNRAVELLING A COMPLEX PATTERN	87
	The Holy Sepulchre	88
	Starck's Clerical	92
	Scenario	93
	Beneath Jerusalem	95
	Secret Codes	98

PART THREE: PROOFS

8	MILES & CUBITS	109
	The Toise & The Templars	113
9	EXPLORATION OF THE CIRCLE	115
	Divine Proportion	119
	Genius Unlocked	123
	Solution to an Ancient Problem	126
10	CONCLUSIONS	129
	Guessing Game	132
	Postscript	139

PART FOUR: CALCULATIONS

11	THE GEOMETRICAL KEY	143
	Definition of the Key	145
	Calculations Co-ordinates	151
	Calculations of Theoretical Co-ordinates within 'System 45 Bornholm'	153
	Comparative Analysis	176
	Chronology	183
	Bibliography	185
	Appendix	
	Corvus – The Raven	187
	Index	191

LIST OF ILLUSTRATIONS

One of the Rennes-le-Château parchments (Henry Lincoln)	6
Standing stones on the north coast of Bornholm (Erling Haagensen)	9
A statue of King Dagobert (Henry Lincoln)	10
Eigil Ragnarsen – a rock on the shore of Bornholm (Erling Haagensen)	12
Crosses and runic inscriptions from Bornholm (Erling Haagensen)	13
Østerlars church *(Bornholmaeldgamle Kirker)*	21
Templar round church in Cambridge	22
Pope Urban II	23
St Helena (Mary Evans Picture Library)	24
Jacques Burgundius de Molay (Mary Evans Picture Library)	26
Entrance to the Virgin's Well *(Underground Jerusalem* by H.Vincent)	28
King Valdemar the Great (Erling Haagensen)	31
Nicholas Breakspear	33
Nylars church *(Bornholmaeldgamle Kirker)*	37
Interior of Bodilsker church (Erling Haagensen)	38
The ground plan of Østerlars church *(Bornholmaeldgamle Kirker)*	43
Plan of Trelleborg *(Bornholms Mysterium)*	46
The round churches of Olsker and Nyker (Erling Haagensen)	48
The massive walls of Østerlars (Erling Haagensen)	49
The original church of Vestermarie *(Bornholmaeldgamle Kirker)*	53
The present church of Vestermarie (Erling Haagensen)	54
Olsker church (Erling Haagensen)	61
A fragment of the letter by Captain Wolfson (Danish State Archive)	63
Bodilsker church and the Devil's Hat (Erling Haagensen)	67
Bornholm and Christiansø with the pentagram overlaid on the map *(Documents of Evolution Danmark S/1)*	67
Title page of *La Vraie Langue Celtique* (Henry Lincoln)	71
Church of the Holy Sepulchre, Jerusalem (The Ancient Art & Architecture Collection Ltd)	89
Title page of *Underground Jerusalem* *(Underground Jerusalem* by H.Vincent)	97
Johan Millén's book (Erling Haagensen)	98
The siege of Jerusalem (Mary Evans Picture Library)	100

The spot where the builders of Hezekiah's tunnel met
   (*Underground Jerusalem* by H.Vincent)   100

The ancient portal to the City of David (*Underground Jerusalem* by H.Vincent)   101

Henrik Juvelius' scribbled notes (Erling Haagensen)   102

The inscription in Hezekiah's tunnel (*Underground Jerusalem* by H.Vincent)   104

The Ark of the Covenant (The Ancient Art & Architecture Collection Ltd)   106

Knudsker church (Erling Haagensen)   116

Klemensker and Rutsker churches (Erling Haagensen)   119

Povlsker and Ibsker churches (Erling Haagensen)   125

Plan of Østerlars and the solstice alignments (Erling Haagensen)   131

Nylars church (Erling Haagensen)   132

The Olsker staircase (Erling Haagensen)   138

A letter from Professor Lind (Erling Haagensen)   144

COLOUR PLATES

between pages 52 and 53

The golden Guldgubbe (Bornholm Museum)

Exterior of Østerlars church (Erling Haagensen)

The solstice sunrise in Østerlars church (Erling Haagensen)

The devil fresco in Østerlars church (Erling Haagensen)

The central pillar at Østerlars church (Erling Haagensen)

Christiansø, the tiny islet to the north of Bornholm (Kai Munch)

The Nylars cross (Erling Haagensen)

between pages 116 and 117

The frescos in Nylars church (Erling Haagensen)

King Charles XIII of Sweden (Sverre Dag Mogstad)

A 19th century engraving of a Knight Templar (Mary Evans Picture Library)

The knights in Østerlars church (Erling Haagensen)

The Holy Grail (Erling Haagensen)

MAPS

12th century Europe   4

The Baltic Sea in the 12th century   32

Hezekiah's tunnel in Jerusalem   103

Mediaeval Europe and the Mediterranean   137

ACKNOWLEDGEMENTS

We acknowledge the invaluable assistance received, over the years, from many people and for which we are deeply grateful.

In particular, we would like to thank:
Hanne Dalgas Christiansen, Leif and Sofia Ekström, Finn Harteg, Niels Lind, Ole Lind, Finn Ole Sonne Nielsen, Jan Petersen, Hanne Risgaard and James R Smith.

Part One
FACTS

**Sapiens nihil affirmat
quod non probet**

(The wise man affirms nothing
which he cannot prove.)

Chapter One
BEGINNINGS

This book is the result of the coming together of what appeared to be two separate quests. Two apparently unconnected pieces of research, fixed upon locations a thousand miles apart, the one on a Danish island in the Baltic Sea, the other in the French foothills of the Pyrenees, proved to be locked in an intimate relationship. Together they have brought to light an astonishing body of lost and forgotten knowledge, skill and expertise once shared by the distant ancestors of our modern civilisation.

Our history teaches us to think of our forebears as living in ignorance, steeped in superstition, lacking our enlightened scientific understanding of the world about us. We consider our knowledge to be the hard-won fruit of generations of thinkers, each building upon the discoveries of preceding ages, learning little by little the wonders and complexities of our universe. It is hard for us to imagine that an unknown and forgotten culture may once have possessed gifts, understanding and learning that were allowed to slip into oblivion and which, painstakingly, we have had to re-learn.

One half of the groundwork for this account began in Denmark, with Erling Haagensen's discovery of some remarkable and unexpected facts; curious facts which seemed not to chime well with our understanding of the past; facts which seemed to be generating a mystery of their own.

Henry Lincoln's half of the work had been a struggle through years of hypothesising in the attempt to unravel a curious and localised historical mystery in France. The end result of that struggle was the confrontation of a body of indisputable facts which left the hypotheses far behind and laid the foundations for yet another struggle; the struggle to understand what had been uncovered.

It was not until time brought the two halves of the quest together that the underlying puzzle began to reveal its breadth and complexity. We shall begin this account, therefore, with brief outlines of the two seemingly widely separated beginnings and the manner in which they were brought together.

*   *   *

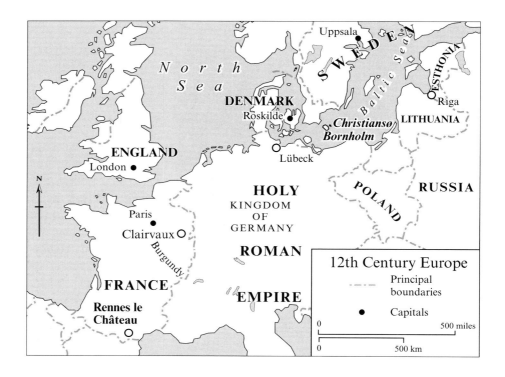

THE PATHWAYS

The Danish half of this quest began as an apparently straightforward attempt to answer an apparently straightforward question. Why were the mediaeval churches on the island of Bornholm unlike any others in Denmark?

This small, but beautiful, island was the birthplace of Erling Haagensen. The history of the community and its traces of an ancient past were inevitably of interest to someone whose ancestors had, for many generations, contributed to the shaping of Bornholm's story. The enigma of the churches - for their origins have long been matters of dispute among historians - seemed a subject clearly worthy of research and undeniably so to someone whose career had led him into the world of journalism and the making of television programmes. Here was interesting material which required investigation and which certainly posed many as yet unanswered questions. Fitting matter for journalistic endeavour and, in this case, of personal interest for the possible light which might be shed upon Erling's own ancestral past.

Delving into the history of the churches soon led to an examination of their relationship with the scattered communities which they served. This, in turn, led to a realisation that the physical placement of the churches held more than a peripheral interest. And thus were made the first steps towards the unexpected discovery that the churches of Bornholm held the key to a greater mystery.

Henry Lincoln, who was working on the French part of the research, was also a writer for television. This was a fortuitous coincidence, which provided the common ground of a shared profession, when the two at last came together. Henry's work had begun with the casual purchase of a paperback book to provide entertainment for an idle holiday hour.

In the 1960s, a French writer, Gérard de Sède, had published this paperback, an entertaining, light-weight account of a strange mystery set in the foothills of the French Pyrenees. It appeared to be no more than a classic treasure-hunt yarn and the basic facts seemed simple. At the end of the nineteenth century, a village priest had apparently become suddenly and inexplicably rich, he must therefore, it seemed, have found a treasure. What was it? Where and how had he found it?

This intriguing mystery eventually led to the production of three documentary films for the BBC - *The Lost Treasure of Jerusalem ...?* (1972), *The Priest, the Painter & the Devil* (1975) and *The Shadow of the Templars* (1978). These were followed by four books - *The Holy Blood and the Holy Grail* (1982)[1], *The Messianic Legacy* (1985)[1], *The Holy Place* (1991) and *Key to the Sacred Pattern* (1997). This almost three decades of research gave the story a world-wide audience. Readers seeking a detailed knowledge of how the research developed will find the groundwork fully detailed in the above works. In them, the puzzle will be seen to move far from the simple question of a possible buried treasure and into the totally unexpected realm of the hunt for a lost body of knowledge.

Briefly encapsulated, the original story told of a priest, Bérenger Saunière, who, in 1891 apparently found four parchments hidden in a hollow pillar which served as support for the altar in his church. The parchments contained secret messages, of which the most illuminating was a concealed geometric form. This seemingly irrelevant clue to the treasure mystery eventually led to the discovery of a rigid and carefully controlled geometric 'structuring' of the landscape around the priest's village of Rennes-le-Château.

The first of the books in which this discovery was recounted, *The Holy Place*, had just been published when the initial contact was made between the two separate parts of the research. Neither writer had been aware of the other's increasingly mysterious findings but, within the first brief moments of comparison of their material, it was evident that each was augmenting and illuminating what the other had revealed. A collaboration was inevitable and as both possessed the professional expertise to make this possible, a filmed documentary series, *The Secret* (1993), was

---

[1] Both co-written with Richard Leigh and Michael Baigent.

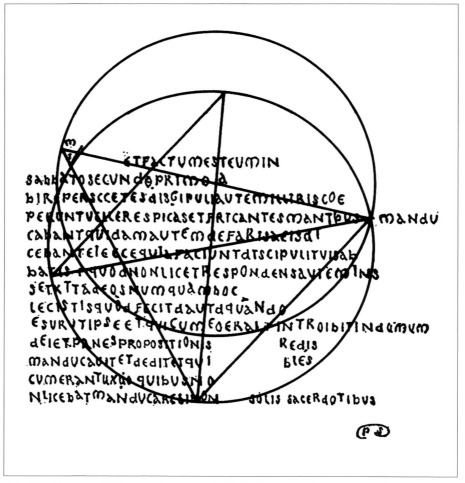

One of the Rennes-le-Château parchments, overlaid with the concealed geometric design.
They were allegedly discovered by Bérenger Saunière in his church in 1891.

made in the months that followed in order immediately to present to the public an overview of the rapidly developing body of material.

The major part of this book will concentrate upon the Danish aspect of the mystery, as the story of the French priest is already sufficiently detailed in the books cited above. The present work is a more comprehensive account of the Bornholm discovery. Both locations will be seen to be sharing, or drawing upon, a common source of lore, scientific knowledge and sophisticated skill. The essential part of what follows is not hypothesis, but is based upon demonstrable data which will be provided so that readers may confirm for themselves the stated facts.

We wish to make it clear that these facts have not been discovered by the present writers – rather, they have been re-discovered. For it will become clear that the knowledge presented in these pages must once have been well-known to our forefathers. Or, at least, to a select body of them. This knowledge, which will seem to be clearly imbued with what we would consider 'modern' expertise, was nevertheless an integral part of the world in which they lived, even though that long-gone world seems now so alien to us. More than anything, we must underline that the reader should not bring the baggage of a 'modern' world-view to the consideration of the labours of these past-masters. For masters, they were, and they inhabited a different universe.

THE OTHER WORLD

We are about to embark upon a real-life mystery in which secrets will be revealed; secrets which it would once have been perilous - even fatal - to disclose. That these matters could, literally, have been dangerous may now seem absurd - especially as they appear to contain an element of what has been labelled 'magic', but which, in fact, is nothing of the kind. Such a word now conjures the innocent 'abracadabra' world of the TV illusionist, which is far from the reality of magic as our ancestors understood it. But 'illusion' is not quite the word to describe what the ancient initiates were doing. Today we substitute the word 'delusion' to explain their arcane beliefs. In a superior and enlightened fashion we lament our ancestors' ignorance – and in this we, too, are deluded.

The secrets disclosed in these pages will uncover an advanced wisdom and insight into nature and its laws which go far beyond anything we have, thus far, believed to be in the possession of our distant forefathers. Before we begin our journey to the shores of a lost and forgotten land, we must make clear that the world inhabited by those forefathers was very different from our own. Certainly, they did not possess our technical skills. But much more important was their totally different way of thinking and their view of the world about them.

First it is necessary to grasp that what we call 'supernatural forces' were not, in any sense, part of superstition, nor were they confined to matters of 'belief'. For our ancestors, such forces were part of reality. Supernatural powers were acknowledged by society by the Church and the State. Angels and devils were real; they populated the world and, indeed, the entire universe. They were not the fictional creations of art and literature, but were integrally part of the systems of justice and science.

It is difficult for us to understand and to accept this world-view. The Inquisition and the witchcraft trials of the Middle Ages seem to us to be incomprehensible. But, for our ancestors, they were founded upon a clear and simple logic. Their 'real' world teemed with supernatural beings, whereas in our 'real' world, such beings, by definition, cannot exist. We have made a world in which their reality no longer functions. Let us provide a seemingly foolish illustration.

On a dark winter's night, you are stopped by the police for cycling without lights. In court, you claim that, of course you had a light on your bike when you left home, but, on the lonely highway you encountered the devil. This creature of darkness, hating the light which guided you, stole it and threatened to bear you away. But you made the sign of the cross and, invoking the aid of the holy Christopher, patron saint of voyagers, you evaded the clutch of the evil one, who disappeared in clouds of sulphurous smoke - but bearing your lamp with him.

In a courtroom of today, you would not have much of a case - even if you produced witnesses to back your story. Your witnesses would probably face their own charges for contempt of court. But, in a mediaeval courtroom, your explanation would have been listened to and considered with gravity. With witnesses, you would more than likely have been acquitted. We have described this scenario as 'foolish'. To the modern world, indeed, it is. But it demonstrates the totally different paradigm which we have to keep before us when considering the world which we are about to explore.

We must begin in the thirteenth century and only by understanding that the supernatural, (and more especially, the divine), was a prime driving force behind the acts of our forebears, shall we be able to create the foundation upon which to set the logic and meaning of our mystery.

Our story takes us first to Bornholm, a remote, windswept and rocky islet in the Baltic Sea, in about the year 1200. Before we finish, our journey will have carried us back several thousand years through time - and to even more interesting places both in Europe and the Middle East. Our excursion will also bring us back to our own time, to cast fresh light upon some of the most important enigmas of modern science. All this will spring from a genuine mystery hidden away upon a tiny speck of land lost in a northern sea.

Chapter Two

THE ENIGMATIC ISLAND

Outside Scandinavia, there are not many people who have heard of Bornholm. An even smaller number have visited its tranquil shores. Yet it is an unique and beautiful island, with huge white sandy beaches to the south and impressive craggy vistas along its northern shore. The coast is dotted with delightful little fishing villages, crenellated by the stacks of smoke-houses where the catch was cured. Inland, tiny hamlets and handsome farm-houses are scattered across a lush and Arcadian landscape. Today, it is a peaceful and attractive place. Those few tourists who come every summer to enjoy the beauties of the island, never sense the true nature of what is before them, nor are they aware of Bornholm's sacred secrets. But the mystery is there for everyone to see, hidden by an ingenious veil of obscurity.

In the year 1200, Bornholm's population was little more than a few thousands, though it already had a long and indeed a significant history. The island has been inhabited for at least ten thousand years, (any traces of earlier occupation which may have existed were totally obliterated by the last Ice Age.) The Bronze Age - 2-3000 BC - has left vestiges of an extremely rich culture. Burials of this period provide eloquent proof of contact with the peoples of the Mediterranean, some two thousand and more miles away; and this was at a time when such long distance travel was, as far as we know, both slow and extremely difficult and dangerous.

The same period saw the erection of more than a thousand standing stones - megaliths of enormous weight which are scattered over the entire island; some are isolated, some stand in groups. Why? Such prehistoric stone monuments are rare

Standing stones on the north coast of Bornholm.
Many hundreds still remain of the thousand or more which were originally erected.

in Scandinavia. What was the purpose behind the raising of these giants in such great numbers and in this particular place? The many standing stones of Bornholm suggest that the island had a special - and it would seem, a religious - importance, at a time of close contact with the cultures of the Middle East, though this must remain speculation.

The very name of Bornholm raises unexpected questions. Holm is an old Danish word for island. Many centuries ago, the island was known as Burgunderland or Burgunderholm, from which the present name derives. The great Danish historian, Saxo Grammaticus, writing in the twelfth century, calls the island Burgunda. There are also references to Burgendaland and Burghundæholm. An even earlier reference to the island dates from the ninth century, in a report to England's King Alfred the Great (c 849 - 899) from a British merchant named Wulfstan. From the Baltic, he writes to the king that: *'thonne Burgendaland væs uns on bæebord, and tha habbat him sylf Cyning.'* ('Burgendaland was to port - and they have their own king.'). The intriguing prefix 'Burgund' seems to be hinting at a link with the dukedom of Burgundy (French: Bourgogne); though a connection between the Burgundians and this rocky islet far to the north, seems at first to be problematical. Perhaps the similarity is no more than coincidental? But mysteries such as this have a way of producing tantalising fragments which may bring substance to an hypothesis - or may simply add to the confusions.

In 1985-6, an extraordinary treasure was unearthed in a field on Bornholm. This consisted of nearly three thousand tiny figures stamped from sheet gold. Barely an

inch in height, they are so minutely detailed that a microscope is needed in order fully to appreciate the delicacy of their craftsmanship. Before this discovery was made, only about a hundred such figures had been found in Scandinavia.

Struck from dies, the Bornholm hoard includes about a hundred different patterns. The most frequently repeated image, of which there are more than fifty examples, is shown on colour plate 1. It depicts a long-haired and regally robed personage, holding a staff or sceptre. The figures have been dated to c 400-600 AD, which is the period when the Merovingians were at the height of their power. These are the 'Long-Haired Kings' who have already

Statue of Dagobert II, last effective king of the Merovingians – the Long-Haired Kings. He was assassinated in December 679 AD.

figured so largely in the French half of our story. According to the Rennes-le-Château parchments, Bérenger Saunière's treasure supposedly belonged to Dagobert II - the last effective king of the Merovingian dynasty of France - who was assassinated in 679 AD.

The tiny gold plates have provided a puzzle for historians. Their purpose is obscure. Certainly they are too small and delicate to have served as coinage or costume decoration. Their use is more likely to have been ritual or votive. Why they should have appeared in such numbers in a field on Bornholm, has yet to be explained. But the possible link with the Merovingians brings them to the heart of our mystery. With the Merovingians we are linked to the line of Davidic succession and the nobility of Burgundy. But one should not make a wished-for connection based upon no more than a tempting possibility. Bornholm cannot be linked to Burgundy on the mere suggestion of uncertain visual imagery, subjectively interpreted from an object which is, itself, of uncertain origin. However, in this case, the unlikely-seeming link is unexpectedly solid and is generally accepted by historians.[2]

The Spanish historian Orosius, in his *Historiæ Adversum Paganos* (c.417 AD) makes it clear that the first Burgundians did, indeed, originate on Bornholm, from whence they later spread and settled along the river Rhine. Orosius tells us that when these Burgundians were defeated by Attila, King of the Huns, they migrated yet further south, conquering an area which straddled the Jura mountains and eventually they occupied most of Southern France. Around the year 530 AD, Burgundy was linked with the Frankish Kingdom, which later divided into Upper and Lower Burgundy. Finally, by the end of the eighth century, the Dukedom of Burgundy was established, and this included the whole of present-day Bourgogne.

During the thirteenth and fourteenth centuries, Burgundy again began to expand northwards and even included the greater parts of Holland and Belgium. At this period, the Duke of Burgundy held his court in the town of Dijon, where the knightly Order of the Golden Fleece was established. This Order was steeped in Christian mysticism, which will be a recurring thread in the pattern of our story. Bornholm will be seen to have connections both with the Christian mystics and with the specific area in the south of France where the Burgundians were settled. These links will become clear, even though written sources are lacking, for this mystery is built upon another sort of evidence. Documents, after all, can be falsified. The proofs of Bornholm's mystery are of a different and more certain nature.

---

[2] See: Gustav Kossinna: *Indogermanischer Forschungen* VII p. 282 ff. - E. Brate: *Svenska Förminnesforeningens Tidskrift* IX 329 f.- Birger Nerman: *Die Herkunft und die frühsten ausvanderungen der Germanen* p 38 f. - L. Schmidt: *Geschichten der deutschen Stämme* I p. 367 - T. E. Karsten: *Die Germanen* p. 78. Gudmund Schütte: *Our Forefathers* I p. 240, II p. 36 ff - Th. Steche: *Altgermanien im Erdkundebuch des Claudius Ptolemäus* p. 100.

In the twelfth century - (the exact date is uncertain) - Bornholm became a province of the Danish crown and Christianity was brought to the pagan island. This is the time at which the first apparent traces of our mystery appear and the key word is Christianity. While the Church may have established itself among the native Bornholmers, they were unlikely to have been particularly impressed. The ancient Nordic Gods, such as Thor and Odin, did not instantaneously lose their appeal for, nor their influence upon, the island's simple peasant fishermen. In a thirteenth century Icelandic Saga - the *Knytlinge Saga,* Bornholm is described as having 'twelve royal farms and fourteen churches'. Such a large number of churches, on so small an island, would seem to suggest that the majority of the islanders were already good Christians. The Saga, however, also recounts the story of one Eigil Ragnarsen - a local chief - and from this account, it seems evident that the Christian virtues were perhaps not yet quite so firmly implanted on Bornholm.

At the beginning of the eleventh century, the *Knytlinge Saga* tells us, the royal estates were administered by a man named Åge. When he died, King Knud the Great, (known also to the English as their King Canute [1016 - 1035]), appointed Eigil Ragnarsen to succeed him. But Bornholm was a long way from the Danish court - and Eigil decided to play the king himself. Surrounded by a large 'court' of his own, he indulged in a life of riotous carousing, which he financed by summer plundering forays around the Baltic shores. It was during one of these pillaging trips that Eigil inadvertently sealed his own fate.

At first, the episode seemed innocent enough. After a particularly hectic sea-battle, Eigil had developed a raging thirst - but the water-barrels on his ship had been shattered. The drinking water had collected below deck, where it had mixed with the blood of the wounded. Eigil dipped his helmet into the

This rock, on the shore of Bornholm, is known to the islanders as 'The Head of Eigil Ragnarsen'.

water and drank deep. The bloodstained water dripped from his beard ... he made a truly terrifying sight. A report of this - literally bloodthirsty - incident reached the ears of King Knud, who immediately sent a message to Eigil. To drink human blood (apart, of course, from that of Christ), was, in the eyes of the church, an unquestionable heresy. Eigil was ordered to seek out a priest forthwith and confess his unchristian sin.

Crosses and runic inscriptions from Bornholm. The Bodilsker stones echo the Cross of the Knights Templar. Top row – Bodilsker church. Bottom row – (l) Nylars church; (c) Østerlars church; (r) Vestermarie church.

Eigil, however, had no time for priests, who disapproved of his summer raping and pillaging jaunts. They even disapproved of his drunken mid-winter binges which, after all, were held in honour of God (or rather, the gods Thor and Odin). Eigil ignored the king's order. But when Knud later heard that a merchant ship belonging to one of his relatives - the Earl of Norway - had been plundered and burned in the Baltic, his patience came to an end. He made a sudden dash to Bornholm, arrested Eigil and summarily hanged him from the highest tree on the island. The story seems to imply that Christianity had not yet taken a very firm hold - neither on Eigil nor on the Bornholmers in general.

The continuing strength and persistence of the old religion is, strangely, confirmed by finds made in a very early Christian cemetery, dating from the time of the incidents referred to in the *Knytlinge Saga*. To all outward appearance, the cemetery is Christian - the graves, for instance, being oriented east-west in accordance with church practice. But the graves also contain small offerings and tokens which relate clearly to the after-life of Nordic myth. The Christian dead seem to have carried their pagan beliefs with them into the world beyond.

Evidence of churches and churchyards can be found in Scandinavia from the very earliest days of the introduction of Christianity, at the end of the first millennium. The first churches were of wood, to be followed later by stone constructions. Curiously, no trace of a wooden church has ever been found on Bornholm - and the earliest churchyard is remote from the surviving stone structures. Perhaps this cemetery was once attached to a wooden church, now disappeared without trace? Why then was no stone church built on this spot - as is normal elsewhere in Denmark? Is it possible that the very unusual stone churches of Bornholm conform to their own particular placement system, dictated by other and specific criteria? And, if so, what might these criteria be? To answer these questions we must join the pathway at its very beginning.

BORNHOLM'S CHURCHES

The *Knytlinge Saga* tells us that Bornholm had fourteen churches. Whether this was the number in existence at the time of Eigil, or two centuries later, when the Saga was written, is unclear. We know, however, that mediaeval Bornholm saw the eventual erection of fifteen very strange stone churches, three of which were pulled down and rebuilt on the same sites at the end of the nineteenth century. One other of the mediaeval churches is now no more than a ruin. But eleven of the fifteen original buildings are still in use today. These churches form the core of our investigation.

The fifteen stone churches of Bornholm are unlike any others in Denmark. Four of them are round and nowhere in the world is there such a high concentration of round churches - apart, that is, from Jerusalem. The curiosity of these four circular structures lies in the arrangement of choir and apse, related directly to a cylindrical rotunda; the three forming interacting horizontal circles. The vault of the rotunda is supported by a single, massive central pillar. Architecturally, these round buildings have no parallel in Denmark. There is, however, one precise match for this design. It is to be found in the chapel of a famous stronghold of the Middle Ages - Château Pèlerin at Athlit in Palestine, built by the great Order of mediaeval fighting monks, the Knights Templar. Most Templar architecture is reminiscent of this unique building style. It can, for instance, be seen clearly in the Order's church 'Convento de Christo' at Tomar in Portugal.[3]

---

[3] Mette Wivel, *Bornholms Runde Kirker og Tempelriddderne*, Bornholmske Samlinger, III raekke, 3 bind (1989)

Apart from the curiosity of the four circular constructions, all the Bornholm churches are accompanied by unusual towers, which will also require examination. This unique strangeness of church design on the island raises two inevitable questions:

1: What was the purpose of the design?

2: Where did the design originate?

These questions have long been the subject of historical debate and controversy. The plan suggests that the buildings were not intended solely for the worship of Christ, but had an additional - and probably defensive - military purpose. The main hypothesis current among historians is the conventional one, that the religious buildings also provided refuge for the local population in time of danger. Indeed, at the time of their construction in the twelfth century, Denmark was suffering continual raids along its Baltic coastline by the piratical Slavonic Wends, who held the formidable bastion of Arkona on the island of Rügen, off the German coast. However these attacks were brought to a definitive end in 1169, when the Danish King Valdemar I (the Great), conquered Rügen and burned Arkona to the ground. Thereafter, and for the remainder of the twelfth and thirteenth centuries, the Baltic coastline was at peace, and there was no further need for the building of defensive fortresses. It follows, that if their purpose was defensive, then the Bornholm churches must pre-date 1169.

This has been a major part of the dispute between historians, since strong arguments have been made in favour of a post- and not pre-1169 date. Certainly, it can be maintained that some of the structures may date from a decade or so later, when peace was still uncertain and had not been definitively established. However, it is generally supposed that the churches are most unlikely to have been built any later than the first half of the thirteenth century. The correct dating of these churches is of extreme importance. If they can be proven to post-date 1169, then some other explanation than defence must be found for their unusual design.

GOTHIC ARCHITECTURE

Mathias Bidstrup, the Danish architect, in his important record of the Bornholm churches,[4] emphasises that their architecture demonstrates a fusion of both romanesque and gothic elements. This suggests that, for this part of the world, the earliest possible construction date must be the beginning of the thirteenth century.

The gothic features are, in themselves, extremely interesting. Could there be any link with the great gothic cathedrals of mediaeval Europe? The cathedrals, it is said, were built by the 'free' masons - that is, builders who were initiated into specific

---

[4] Bidstrup, M., *Bornholms Middelalderlige Kirker,* Bornholmske Samlinger 7, 1912.

guild secrets, among which was such arcane knowledge as the dimensions of King Solomon's Temple in Jerusalem. These 'free masons' supposedly travelled about the continent, building cathedrals which were based upon secret measures and relationships. It is impossible to say how much truth there may be in these tales, but it is certain that the cathedrals share a characteristic and collective symbolic language in their decoration, which can easily be recognised by the trained eye. Incorporated into their very architecture, abstruse and mysterious elements were hidden, it seems, from the uninitiated laity.

The gothic is an extraordinary and original architectural style, which appeared suddenly in France around the year 1130, born whole and entire and with no apparent development or experimentation. (*En passant*, we must note that it was in 1127 that the Knights Templar returned from Jerusalem and reported to their mentor, Bernard of Clairvaux, that their 'mission' - whatever that might have been - was 'accomplished'. There is thus a link in time between the Templars and the first appearance of the gothic style.) Within a very short span of time, the gothic reached its climax. The cathedrals multiplied - astonishing marvels of architecture, demonstrating an extremely advanced knowledge of engineering, mathematics and geometry. In less than a hundred years, eighty similar wonders were constructed. At the time of the building of Chartres Cathedral, nearly twenty other such masterpieces were under construction in northern France alone. How was such a burst of original creative endeavour achieved? Whence came the expertise? How were so many skilled architects, master craftsmen, artisans and builders found within so relatively small an area?

As the burgeoning of the gothic is considered, the questions multiply. How did this astonishing innovation appear at the same time and in so many places throughout the Christian west? It seems, for instance, virtually impossible to say where the first ogive vault was erected, as they seem to have appeared simultaneously all over Europe. Just as mysterious is the financing of the work. The town of Chartres had only a few thousand inhabitants. How could such a modest community have funded the construction of so enormous and sublime an edifice as the cathedral of *Notre Dame?* One must wonder, too, how the poor, remote and isolated fishing community of Bornholm could expend so much of its energy and resources on the construction of so many, albeit more modest, churches.

One seems driven to the conclusion that a well-organised plan was being put into operation. But - by whom? And now we have a question which appears to provide the glimpse of an answer. Above all, the gothic style appears in the abbeys of the Cistercians. In his book on Chartres Cathedral, Louis Charpentier says:

> In order to achieve the gothic vault and all that accompanies it, it was
> necessary ..... to devise nothing less than a descriptive geometry which was
> able to show, in a simple diagram laid out upon the ground, not only the
> interrelationships of volume, upright and curve, but also the accord of thrust

and counter-thrust. All this by the simple play of geometric and harmonic forces. This science ..... at least in its material aspect, was taught to the constructors of religious buildings by the monks of Citeaux. These 'missionaries of the gothic' as Pierre de Colombier called them.[5]

This description of the Cistercians seems apposite. Later in this book we shall have cause to examine the life of the leading figure of these 'missionaries of the gothic', Bernard of Clairvaux. It will clearly be seen that, both in his contacts as well as in his organisational abilities, he was more than capable of the conception and financing necessary for the mammoth undertaking of the construction of the gothic cathedrals. Indeed, it is hard to imagine anyone more capable of the task. With the skills, abilities and wealth of both Cistercians and Templars directly under his control, he had access to the scientific knowledge, the funds and the talent of the society in which he lived. And the Orders which he controlled displayed yet another and essential talent - that of secretiveness - or, at the least, discretion.

The very word 'gothic' merits examination. This totally new and 'scientific' building method, facilitated the creation of immensely impressive stone structures. Arches could now be constructed to heights which would previously have been considered impossible. The very light could now be made to flow freely through vast rose windows. Such buildings, as they began to tower over their mediaeval surroundings, must have been awe-inspiring and seemed well nigh miraculous, to the townsfolk who huddled at their feet in their little timber and wattle-and-daub houses. But why should this new development, which made such skilful use of the interaction between the laws of geometry and gravity, be called gothic art?

The question has no certain answer. It has been suggested that the word has no connection with the Goths, but is derived from the Greek 'goetik', meaning 'magical'. Another interesting suggestion has been made by the French alchemist, Fulcanelli, in his book *Le Mystère des Cathédrales*. (Fulcanelli disappeared in mysterious circumstances in 1925. The book was later published by Eugène Canseliet.) Fulcanelli points out that *art gothique* (gothic art) can be interpreted as an orthographic transcription of the word *argothique*. *Art goth = argot* - which means 'slang' - (originally a secret language used by criminals). A dictionary definition of 'slang' is: 'the specialised language of a particular class of people,' - a language only comprehensible to those 'in the know' i.e., the Initiated.

According to the Greek myth of Jason, *argot* was the language spoken by the argonauts - the crew of the ship Argo, which was built by Argos. Under the leadership of Jason, the ship and its crew sailed out to find the Golden Fleece on the 'happy coasts of Kolchis'. Suddenly, our attention is drawn back to Burgundy. A faint echo crosses the silent centuries. The mythical Greek 'Golden Fleece' is

[5] Louis Charpentier: *Les mystères de la cathédrale de Chartres*, Laffont 1966 (p 55)

rediscovered in the initiatory chivalric Order at the Burgundian court, as the *art gothique* begins to spread and flourish in the Christian west.

Both Fulcanelli and the myths of Ancient Greece link the name 'gothic' with language. So - what is language? A language consists of words – sound symbols with specific meanings. The symbols make it possible for us to communicate with each other. When we know the meaning of the symbols, we can understand the language. The symbols used in the architecture of the Gothic cathedrals can be described as an archetypal geometry, and these same symbols are to be found in religious structures around the world.

But before we become immersed in the apparently daunting arcana of geometric symbolism, it is necessary to dwell for a moment upon this crucial element of our investigation. It is important that the reader should understand that a knowledge of geometry is in no way necessary in order to grasp the significance of the symbols with which we are about to deal. (The detailed explanations required by those versed in such matters have been confined to Chapter 11)

However, a simple yet basic property of geometry must now be explored, as it explains why the symbols linked with religious architecture are geometric. It is the key to the 'language' which we are trying to understand. Fortunately, the explanation is simple: the ideas are basic, and they are not new. Indeed, even though they seem new and original to most people today – they were well known in the past.

THE MAGIC OF NUMBER

One of the most important of the elements in the language of symbolic geometry is the square within the circle:

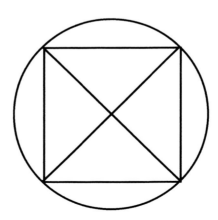

Consider the simple elements of this symbol. The square has four sides of equal length. It has two diagonals (the lines connecting its opposite corners), which are also of equal length. Touching each of the four corners of the square is the circumference of its enclosing circle. Thus, it can clearly be seen that the elements of the symbol are of three categories: the side, the diagonal and the circumference. And therein lies the significance - for these three categories symbolise a basic understanding of the construction of the universe. But before this can be explained we must consider one of the most incomprehensible and mysterious riddles ever to be found in nature. And this is to do with measure.

Normal human logic suggests that it should be possible to measure everything. A line, once drawn, can be measured. This - it would seem - should be a relatively simple task. The surprising truth is, however, that nature is so constructed that, in certain respects, this is virtually impossible. If, for instance, the side of a square is measured - in inches, feet, yards, metres or any other unit of measure - then that particular unit cannot precisely define the length of its diagonal. This can be mathematically proven, even though the concept seems difficult to grasp in terms of simple, unmathematically-educated, human logic. In geometry, this problem has been solved by the invention of a new number system which is 'parallel' to the usual numbers. These new numbers are referred to as square roots (as they are derived from squares). In the case of a square whose side measures one unit, the diagonal measures precisely the square root of two - written as $\sqrt{2}$.

Since this new system seems to run counter to our normal human logic, the numbers have been labelled 'irrational', in contrast to normal numbers which are considered to be 'rational'. But the mystery does not end here. There is yet one more family of numbers which are neither 'rational' nor 'irrational', but 'transcendental'. In face of such concepts, the mathematically untrained brain begins to find itself groping in a fog of non-comprehension. However, at least one of these transcendental numbers is not totally unfamiliar to the layman. We have all heard of 'pi' - written as the Greek letter π - even if our grasp of its significance fades as our schooldays recede. We probably remember that it has something to do with measuring the circumference of a circle. In fact, this transcendental number is necessary, as neither rational nor irrational numbers can define with exactitude either the circumference or the area of a circle. Here are yet more mysteries for the human mind to grapple with - but nevertheless they are factual.

Consider again the symbol in the Figure on page 18 - the square within the circle. This symbol represents, in the simplest possible way, the three different families of numbers which create and measure everything in the universe. The three families cannot unite. In the language of the mathematician, they are 'incommensurate' with each other. This symbolic construct is to be found across the world - in Greek temples and Egyptian pyramids; in Muslim mosques and Jewish synagogues; in sacred buildings in India, Japan, China and South America. One may therefore conceive that it has been used deliberately by the constructors to represent something which, from one standpoint is incommensurable - impossible to unify - yet from another may certainly, in the human mind, be united: the earthly and the divine. Sacred architecture can therefore be considered to symbolise the union of the apparently incompatible, in a building which is created for the earthly adoration of the divine.

Irrational numbers were certainly known to the ancient Greeks. The knowledge possessed by such mathematicians as Pythagoras, Euclid and Archimedes has survived and been handed down. But, consider for a moment, what might have happened if a disaster had struck the records of ancient Greek culture - a disaster such as the destruction of the library at Alexandria. Had the record been wiped clean of the works of Pythagoras or Euclid, we would not now be aware of their astonishing - and vital - legacy.

Curiously, historians seem to cling to the idea that human knowledge, once acquired, cannot be lost. For them, ancient civilisations cannot have possessed knowledge unknown to the modern world. But there is exceptionally strong evidence to the contrary. Do not those same historians, themselves, regret and wonder what precious learning might have perished in the flames of Alexandria? This suggestion of ancient 'lost' knowledge will prove to be the gateway to an understanding of the mystery which this book attempts to confront. It can be glimpsed in the geometric symbolism of the gothic cathedrals.

It is more than interesting that this same hidden language can be seen in Bornholm's mediaeval churches. We cannot make a direct comparison between the cathedrals and the Bornholm churches - they are far too modest. Nevertheless, there are very many details which make it clear that an 'initiated' geometer was involved in their construction. A first - and clearly evident - fact is that four of Bornholm's churches are round. Their ground plans show three circles. Three of the churches are built on three levels - (the fourth seems to have lost its upper floor in the remote past.)

The circular form and the repetition of the number three in both height and length, suggest that the churches may have been built in accordance with the sacred and geometric tradition. Certainly, there is an unmistakable congruence with the architecture found in specifically Templar constructions.

Templar round churches are to be found in England - at Cambridge, Dover, Northampton and London. In France there are those of D'aiguilhe near to Le Puy, Fontevrault, Laon, Metz, Montmajour, Montmorillon and Paris. In Spain are Eunate, Segovia and Torres del Rio. Portugal, of course, has Tomar - the best preserved of all the Templar churches.

Like the round churches of Bornholm, Tomar is both church and fortress - just as the Knights Templar were both monks and warriors who built *capelli militium* - military chapels. The architecture of the church of Tomar is also special. It has a

Østerlars church

The Round Church; or Church of the Holy Sepulchre, Cambridge

central pillar, which is itself built of arches to enclose yet another central, circular space. This design is unique to the Templars - with the single and notable exception of Bornholm's round church at Østerlars (See colour plate).[6] The striking similarities of construction make it unlikely that the links are no more than coincidental. But is it possible that the Templars could have played any part in the history of the Baltic? There appears to be no record of any active involvement of the Order in this part of the world. Nevertheless, as we explore the fundamental secrets attached to these fighting monks, we shall uncover cryptic evidence which does more than hint at such a possibility.

[6] Mette Wivel, *Bornholms Runde Kirker og Tempelridderne,* Bornholmske Samlinger, III række, 3. bind (1989).

Chapter Three

SECRETS OF THE KNIGHTS TEMPLAR

In the year 1095, Pope Urban II called a Church Council at Clermont in France. There was nothing unusual about the summoning of such Councils, they were held on a regular basis by the Catholic Church. The Council of Clermont, however, was different. The usual clerical authorities were, of course, present. But this time the Pope had decided to invite the major part of the French nobility and gentry. He wished to present them with an idea. An idea which might solve what had become a substantial problem concerning pilgrimages to the Holy Land - and in particular, to the Church of the Holy Sepulchre in Jerusalem. Such pilgrimages were looked upon as holy and proper Christian works - even though Jerusalem was in the hands of the Muslim Arabs.

In the past, the Arabs had not placed any barriers in the way of Christian pilgrims, who had access to all the holy places in return for the payment of a fee. For the Arabs, this was simply a matter of good business. As long as the Christians were prepared to pay, then they were well treated, but by 1095, things had changed. Jerusalem had been taken by the Turks, whose attitude was completely different; they simply wished the Christians to disappear - literally. Indeed, the whole of Christianity's Eastern Empire was in danger of falling to Islam.

Not surprisingly the Pope considered this new state of affairs to be a serious problem. At the Council of Clermont, he delivered a very strong and emotional speech. In vivid language, he described the

Pope Urban II (1088-1099), called the First Crusade at the Council of Clermont, 1095.

misery and sufferings which were then being inflicted upon the Christian pilgrims in Palestine. At the end of a long and distressing account, the Pope announced that God would grant total absolution for all sins, both present and to come, to any knight who would put his life in jeopardy in the cause of the liberation of Jerusalem from the cruel, sadistic, brutal and inhuman pagans.

There is no question of the power of the Pope's words on all those who were present. Three years later, when the Christian knights forced their way into Jerusalem, they knew that there would be no meting out of heavenly retribution for their excesses: God had already absolved them of their sins. The rape and the butchery were merciless and the greater part of the Muslim inhabitants were slaughtered in furthering the desire of the church to liberate the city. And this desire was built upon the idea of a longed-for 'Kingdom of God'.

Throughout the first millennium AD, many of the faithful had clung to the idea that Christ would return to establish his Kingdom on Earth after a thousand years. But the year one thousand had come and gone without the expected glorious Second Coming. The faithful had begun to wonder what was amiss. The idea began to grow that perhaps Christ could not return as long as his Holy Sepulchre remained in infidel hands.

The location of this Holy Sepulchre, it should be noted, had been unknown until the year 326 AD, when it had been identified by Helena, the mother of the Roman Emperor Constantine. One cannot help but wonder how, after 300 years of oblivion, the exact location of Jesus' burial place had been so readily rediscovered by the Emperor's mother. Helena, we are told, had been led by intuition - and a dream. But, as we shall later see, there may be an undercurrent to this legend which could be hinting at something more conscious and logical.

St Helena (248-328), mother of the Emperor Constantine the Great. In a dream, or vision, she 're-discovered' the tomb of Jesus and the True Cross.

According to the Bible, (Matt.27, 57-60) the body of Jesus had been placed in a 'new tomb ... hewn out of the rock' and which belonged to Joseph of Arimathea.

It has been suggested that Helena was, in fact, a descendant of Joseph of Arimathea[7] and may, therefore have inherited family knowledge of the sepulchre. However, once such unprovable suggestions as a link between Helena and Joseph of Arimathea are adopted, then the door is opened for the posing of any number of - more or less likely - questions. Could it be, for example, that Helena was in possession of family secrets, kept by the descendants of Joseph of Arimathea? Could it be that her mission - made possible by her son's position - required free and undisturbed access to the area, in order to rescue a precious 'something' which her forefather, Joseph of Arimathea, had concealed?

---

[7] Laurence Gardner: *The Bloodline of the Holy Grail,* Element Books, 1996. pp 313-314.

In this context, it is worth noting that in secret societies, such as the Knights Templar or Freemasons, there is alleged to be a tradition of keeping the most precious secrets in a coffin, buried in a secret vault, associated with the Grand Master's grave. With this additional possibility, it is but a short step to the suggestion that this tradition had been followed in connection with the burial of Jesus. Thus may be produced the scenario that important documents concerning Jesus' organisation - (assuming he had one) - and in particular his secret knowledge - (assuming he had any) - were buried in, or near, the Holy Sepulchre. Helena's (alleged) vision would now be transformed. She was simply acting upon her (alleged) inherited knowledge in order to recover lost and precious family heirlooms of some kind. Certainly such suppositions seem to put Helena's supposed psychic abilities into a much more apparently realistic context - even though the questions which have created the scenario are based upon nothing more than a hypothetical re-reading of the accounts.

BELIEFS AND HYPOTHESES

We must immediately stress that, of course, this kind of hypothesising, with its elements of unknowable 'secret knowledge', can have no reliably valid substance. Without some vestige of proof, such propositions can only remain in the realm of entertaining conjecture. One must, though, be equally cautious about peremptorily dismissing evidence which people may claim to have. Their evidence *may* be valid. Their stories *may* be true. One simply cannot *know*. To dismiss the claims out of hand, without any consideration, is to show as lamentably naive an attitude as is demonstrated by those who wholeheartedly accept them. The possibilities should, at least, be examined. It is vitally important to remember that, no matter how apparently absurd a proposition may seem to be, some people may once have believed it to be a truth - and perhaps there are some who still cling to such ideas. In order fully to understand the actions of such people, those beliefs must be taken into consideration.

Later in this book, it will be necessary for us to construct, in our turn, an hypothesis. That hypothesis will inevitably, therefore, take into account certain beliefs - some more likely than others - which have been expressed, or implied, by others. They should not be taken as expressions of the present writers' beliefs. Our task is to observe and report. Nor should the reader dismiss even the most doubtful of beliefs without consideration. Neither the reader's opinions, nor ours, are relevant to the strength of another person's faith.

In these doubtful and difficult areas, one is confronting the unavoidable problems of researching into the background of the kind of mystery which this book is attempting to unravel. Like modern Freemasonry, the Templars were, in some sense, a secret Order. Or perhaps more correctly, an Order with secrets. In attempting to delve into their innermost structure, one is inevitably confronted by that wall of secrecy. We simply do not know what if anything may have been the knowledge, the motivation, or the belief system, which they guarded for the sole possession of their initiates.

In this regard, it is worth considering the research undertaken in the late eighteenth century by Charles, the Swedish Duke of Sødermanland (later King Charles XIII of Sweden). He spent most of his life delving into the history of the Templars and his legacy has provided glimpses through some odd and illuminating doors. During his years of research, Charles travelled extensively throughout Europe and amassed what is claimed to be the world's largest collection of literature devoted to such subjects as alchemy - which is today in the possession of the Order of Swedish Freemasons. Also in his library is a work entitled *The Legacy of de Molay,* which relates in detail how the original Order continued clandestinely after the execution of their last Grand Master, Jacques Burgundius de Molay.[8]

Jacques Burgundius de Molay, last Grand Master of the Templars. Burned in Paris in 1314.

Based upon the information he had assembled, Charles created a very curious masonic system, now known as the Swedish System and which is still practised in the countries of Scandinavia. Adherents to this system will therefore be acting in relation to the givens upon which their Order is founded. The opinions of outsiders concerning the validity of those givens must inevitably remain based upon uncertain speculation. This is particularly true, in relation to any material which the Order may keep to itself as privileged, or secret, information.

Certainly, the present authors attach no great or undue significance to these, or other similar, ideas. Neither, however, do we ignore or dismiss them. The beliefs of our ancestors - as well as those of our contemporaries - may strike some of us as odd, or misguided, wrong or lunatic. Nevertheless, beliefs undeniably affect the

[8] Sverre Dag Mogstad: *Frimureri,* Universitetsforlaget, Oslo 1994.

actions of those who hold them. Those actions, in their turn, can and do affect the lives of others who do not hold them. Will anyone deny that the anti-Semitic beliefs of the Nazis had a catastrophic effect upon Jewry in particular and upon the history of the twentieth century in general? Our opinions upon the validity of those beliefs should have no bearing upon our study of their effects.

JERUSALEM

On the location pointed out by his mother, the Emperor Constantine built the *Basilica Passiones vel Sancti Sepulcri* and the church was duly consecrated in the year 326 AD. We are told that the documents held by the Swedish Freemasons assert that it was in this church, in the year 1118, that the nine founding knights swore the oaths which brought the Order of Knights Templar into existence.[9]

With the end of the first millennium, the attention of the Christian world was again focussed on this structure. This was not solely because the Turkish possession of the Holy Land had made pilgrimage an impossible undertaking. There was now the additional, commonly-held and appalling suggestion that the infidels' mere possession of Christ's tomb might be preventing the Second Coming of Jesus and the inauguration of the long-awaited Kingdom of God. Helena's questionable identification of the sacred location had become a given which was to produce far-reaching effects.

In addition to these pressures, there was also the fact that some members of the French aristocracy had another, and stronger, motive of their own. They could lay claim to the throne of the Holy Land as descendants, like Jesus, of the House and Lineage of David. This claim stemmed from their descent from the rulers of the Jewish Princedom which was established in France after the destruction of Jerusalem by the Romans in 70 AD.[10]

For more than sixteen hundred years, countless thousands of Christian pilgrims have knelt in prayer at the site specified by Helena, the mother of Constantine, firmly believing it to be the Tomb of Christ. As, indeed, it may well be - though how can we be certain? Perhaps Helena was in possession of secret knowledge about Joseph of Arimathea's tomb 'wherein was never man yet laid'. It has recently been argued that 'there is ... no compelling reason to believe that the location of the tomb was ever forgotten.'[11] Even so, that there may, indeed, still be secrets hidden beneath the ancient city of Jerusalem cannot seriously be doubted. The Holy Land can be seen as one vast archaeological site, where the digging of the foundations

[9] Dag Mogstad: op. cit.
[10] See: A.J. Zuckerman, *A Jewish Princedom in Feudal France*, New York 1972 and *The Holy Blood and the Holy Grail* pp 412 et seq.
[11] Prof J. Strange – *Theology & Politics in Architecture & Iconography*, Aarhus University Press, 1991.

for a new building, or even the turning of a spade in the sandy soil, can uncover the unexpected. The discovery of the Dead Sea Scrolls caused an explosion in scholarship whose reverberations have not yet faded.

Another such discovery, though less dramatic and thus less well-known, was made in the early years of the twentieth century. From 1909 to 1911, a Swedish scholar named Johan Millén laboured beneath Jerusalem to clear the tunnel which leads water from the Spring of Gihon to the Pool of Siloam. Millén later revealed that he had a secret agenda. The true purpose of his expedition was based upon some remarkable evidence assembled by a Finnish historian, one Henrik Juvelius and would, Millén claimed, lead to the recovery of the lost

Entrance to the 'Virgin's Well' (also known as the Spring of Gihon), Jerusalem. The spring feeds the Pool of Siloam, through the tunnel built by Hezekiah.

Ark of the Covenant. In this aim he was encouraged by the fact that the cleared tunnel led, as Juvelius's indications had promised, to yet another and hidden complex of passageways. The Great War, however, interrupted his excavations and he was never allowed to recommence work. Nor was he ever given the opportunity to explore his newly-discovered hidden passages. Later in this book, there will be cause to examine this extraordinary undertaking more closely.

But there had been earlier excavators beneath the Temple Mount, and furthermore, as with Helena seven hundred years earlier and Millén nine hundred years later, there seems to have been a hidden agenda behind the desire of certain of the Christian knights of the Crusades to gain undisturbed access to the holy sites. These earlier delvers in the ground were the original nine founding knights of the Order of Knights Templar.

Those mysterious nine men spent nine uninterrupted years in clearing the 'Stables of Solomon' beneath the Temple Mount. For the first nine years of their Order's existence, there is no evidence of any kind that the nine knights even attempted to undertake their supposed - and impossible - task, the protection of all the pilgrim highways to the Holy Places of Palestine. On the other hand, it is known that they cleared the so-called 'Stables'. When their first Grand Master, Hugues de Payens, returned to Europe after those significant nine years, he reported to Bernard of Clairvaux that 'their task had been accomplished.' What task? Certainly not the protection of pilgrims. The Stables of Solomon are located beneath the south-eastern corner of the Temple Mount, some three hundred metres from the Spring of Gihon. It is tempting to imagine the Templars finding their way, like Millén, into a labyrinth of unknown tunnels and unearthing who knows what secrets.

But conjecture is not the purpose of this investigation - entertaining though it may be. Nevertheless, it is worth considering the activities of the Templars and the influence upon them of their *eminence grise* - the great Cistercian, Bernard of Clairvaux. An examination of the *dramatis personae* of those involved in the foundation of both Templars and Cistercians, will show the clear linking of both Orders to the nobility of the Dukedom of Burgundy - and significantly, to the island of Bornholm.

ST BERNARD OF CLAIRVAUX

Bernard was born into an aristocratic Burgundian family in 1090 at Fontaines near Dijon, capital of Burgundy. Not only did he stem from a rich and noble line, but legend tells us that a destiny of greatness was foretold for him at his birth.[12] He was educated with the utmost care and at an early age was recognised as being extremely gifted. He seems to have sensed that he was, in some way, 'chosen' and his family certainly shared this idea. In 1113, at the age of twenty-three, Bernard sought admission to the Abbey of Citeaux, the first monastery of the Cistercian Order, whose establishment had been financed by the Duke of Burgundy, Eudes I. The Burgundian nobility seemed unquestionably to be deeply involved in the Order's creation. The Abbot of Citeaux was *ex officio* Prime Counsellor of the Burgundian Parliament with the right to sit at the assembly of the States General of the Kingdom, as well as of the Province of Burgundy.

When Bernard entered the Cistercian Order at Citeaux, he did not join alone. Thirty other of the highest nobles of the province, including Bernard's own father, his five brothers, and many uncles and cousins were also accepted. This seems like a massive intrusion into what was a relatively minor order. Indeed, it almost seems to have more the nature of a take-over. There can be no doubt, however, that Bernard was now part of a small and select Order with extraordinary political power. Two years later, Bernard and his followers were allowed to leave Citeaux and found their own establishment at Clairvaux, on land especially donated by the Count of Champagne, an early recruit to the Templar Order.[13] At the age of twenty-five, Bernard was made Abbot. Only two more years were to pass before the Templars were founded in Jerusalem.

[12] M. Gildas, *St Bernard of Clairvaux*, Catholic Encyclopaedia, 1913.
[13] See *HBHG* p.38 et seq.

When Bernard had joined the Cistercians, they were an impoverished order and Citeaux was their only monastery. By the time of his death in 1153, the order had grown in wealth and power, with more than three hundred monasteries spread throughout the length and breadth of Europe. This impressive growth makes a remarkable parallel with that of the Templars - whose rule is based upon that of the Cistercians. Key figures in both Orders are clearly linked to the same group of Burgundian nobility. They would seem to be the two sides of the same coin. One of his uncles, André de Montbard, was among the nine founding members of the Templar Order. It was to Bernard that Hugues de Payens brought the news of their successful mission in Jerusalem. And it was Bernard who gave the Templars their Rule. In 1128, at the Council of Troyes, the Pope bestowed upon Bernard the resonant title of 'Protector' of the Templar Order and during his lifetime, the Order was secure in its relationship with the Church.

Although the Templars appeared to be controlled by their Grand Master, who was based in Jerusalem, there seems little doubt that Bernard and the Burgundian nobility close to him, were the prime movers in the Order's early years. He can be seen as the real - if covert - Grand Master of the Templars, just as he was clearly the leading figure of the Cistercians. To the very end of his life, he was deeply involved in planning for the future of his two 'children', the Cistercians and the Templars.

But how does Denmark - and more especially the island of Bornholm - become involved in this apparently very French story?

THE SCANDINAVIAN LINK

It is hardly surprising that the history of Denmark is almost unknown outside Scandinavia, or that the history of little Bornholm is even less known. Denmark is a small, peaceful, and completely un-imperialistic democracy and, for centuries, has played no great part in the macro-politics of Europe. But it was not always so. Denmark can take pride in being the world's oldest existing monarchy and, in her long story, she once had ambitions to compete with Europe's greatest empires in the struggle for political power and influence.

In Winchester Cathedral, the tomb of King Knud (Canute) bears witness to this fact. He was the great-grandson of King Gorm, founder of the Danish royal house. Knud conquered England in 1016 - and at his death in 1035, he ruled over Denmark, England and Norway - as well as parts of Sweden and Scotland. Denmark's king was thus among the mightiest rulers of Europe. However, a mere thirty years later, after the Battle of Hastings in 1066, England was lost. By the time of the Crusades, in the twelfth century, when our mystery begins, the kings of Denmark had turned their imperial ambitions from West to East. From England to Denmark's closer and more natural strategic sphere of influence, the Baltic.

In the Baltic, Denmark was forced to compete with the growing influence of Germany, though her lack of the necessary power made military success unlikely. Denmark's ingenuity lay in employing the power of the Church. From as early as the end of the eleventh century, Danish kings had been attempting to persuade the papacy that Denmark should not be, as it then was, administered by the German Archbishopric of Hamburg/ Bremen. Eventually, in 1104, the Pope granted the establishment of an archbishopric in the Danish, (now Swedish), town of Lund. The Archbishop of Lund is to play a key role in our story. A military alliance was to be forged between the Danish king, the archbishop and the legendary Knights Templar, involving a mission to the Baltic Sea - and to the little island of Bornholm.

We can now begin to fix the mystery of Bornholm into an historical framework - and the events of history will provide a logical answer to our earlier questions In these political manoeuvrings will lie the explanation for the curious structure of the Bornholm churches. We shall also find that they have a much more complex role to play - and that role is directly connected to the Templars.

The originator, in the mid twelfth century, of the pact between the Church and the State of Denmark was King Valdemar I, known as Valdemar the Great. His early years were turbulent, tainted with the blood and treachery of internecine strife. For

a long period, the royal inheritance had passed between brothers, thus creating numerous family branches, each of which could lay some sort of claim to the crown. Only days before Valdemar's birth, his own father, Knud Lavard, had been brutally murdered by a nephew in a bid for the throne. The upbringing of the fatherless infant Valdemar was entrusted to the noble family of Hvide (White), which had just produced twin sons. Thus Valdemar grew to manhood blessed with the closeness and support of two 'brothers' - one of whom, Absalon, entered the church and eventually became Bishop of Roskilde, an important Danish town. Later, he was to assume the Archbishopric of Lund.

At Valdemar's accession, Denmark was effectively divided into three kingdoms, two of which were ruled by his cousins, Sven and Knud and the third by Valdemar himself. In 1157 the three

King Valdemar the Great of Denmark, leader of the Baltic Crusade.

31

cousins met in Roskilde, ostensibly to discuss a future peaceful pattern of co-existence. But, at the banquet to celebrate the pact, armed henchmen of Sven broke into the festivities and attacked Knud and Valdemar. Knud was killed, but Valdemar escaped in the confusion. Valdemar then raised an army and defeated the treacherous Sven. His victory assured him the throne of a united Denmark. From then on, Valdemar the king and Absalon, his sworn brother, the Bishop of Roskilde, worked together in a close military and political union for the future growth and well-being of the kingdom.

One of their actions, important because it established a pattern for their future joint enterprises, was the capture of the island of Rügen, just off the present German coast. (See map above) The inhabitants were pagan Wends, given to plundering the Danish shore and carrying off Christian Danes into slavery. Denmark had made numerous attempts to put an end to their depredations and Valdemar made the task the first priority of his reign. In achieving this aim, Valdemar and Absalon brought Christianity to the Wends. Eskil, the Danish Archbishop of Lund, was also personally involved in this action and thus the Church demonstrated its official sanction for the enterprise. He was another member of the Hvide family, and so had close personal and familial links with the king and Bishop Absalon.

Eskil is key to the involvement of the Knights Templar in our story. He had developed an extremely close relationship with Bernard of Clairvaux. After Eskil became Archbishop of Lund in 1137, there followed a very rapid spread of Bernard's Order throughout Denmark. Cistercian monasteries were founded at Alvastra and Nydalal in 1143, Herrevad in 1144, Esrom in 1154, Vitskøl in 1158 and Sorø in 1161. The Danish monasteries were instrumental in the founding of many other Cistercian establishments along the southern Baltic shore: Dargun in 1172; Kolbatz in 1173; Olivia in 1186 and Eldena in 1188.[14] This activity is of crucial significance, as it demonstrates the clear links between the Cistercians and Templars in a large number of joint missions with the Danish throne.

Eskil and St Bernard maintained their contact through lengthy correspondence. Eskil, in fact, had a strong wish to join Bernard's Cistercians and made a visit to Clairvaux in 1152, with the object of obtaining his friend's permission to be admitted to the Order. Bernard, however persuaded him against it, insisting that Eskil had more important work to do at home. This was to be their last meeting, in the following year, Bernard died. But, during his last months, he oversaw a lasting and significant legacy. His Templars, who were at the peak of their power, elected a new Grand Master. This was Bertrand de Blanchefort, who was to prove the most effective of all the Templars' leaders, bringing them firmly onto the stage of international diplomacy.[15] One can sense Bernard's hand at work both in this election and most clearly in his influence upon Archbishop Eskil.

On his return to Denmark, Eskil brought with him a large contingent of Cistercian monks from Clairvaux in order to establish the monastery at Esrom -

Nicholas Breakspear, the only English pope (1154-1159). Friend of Eskil.

unquestionably in accord with Bernard's planning for the future. Three years later, however, Eskil was to be involved in the serious rift between the pope and Frederick Barbarossa, the Holy Roman Emperor, which was also to have unfortunate consequences upon his relationship with the Danish king.

Among Eskil's other significant contacts was the English cardinal, Nicholas Breakspear, who had been appointed papal legate to Scandinavia in 1152. The two men were closely associated at a time of difficulty for the church in the area. It was Breakspear who had to reconcile Eskil to the loss from his jurisdiction of Norway, which had been agitating to be granted its own archbishop.

[14] Friedrich Benninghoven, *Der Orden der Schwertbrüder–Fratres Milicie Christi de Livonia*, Böhlau Verlag, Köln Graz, 1956 (P16).
[15] See *HBHG* p 91 and *passim*.

At the same time, Emperor Frederick Barbarossa was pressing for the abolition of Eskil's archbishopric of Lund and the re-absorption of the Danish church by the See of Hamburg/Bremen. 1153 was to be the crucial year.

When the news of Bernard's death reached him, Eskil set off on a pilgrimage to his friend's grave at Clairvaux. It was at this time that Barbarossa's pressure was mounting upon the octogenarian Pope Anastasius IV. When, in December 1154, the pope died, the Church, within twenty-four hours, appointed a stronger man to succeed him. This was Eskil's friend, the Englishman Nicholas Breakspear, who was elected as Adrian IV. Eskil immediately went to Rome, where Adrian ratified his status as archbishop. This was not what Barbarossa wanted. On his way home, Eskil was seized as he passed through Burgundy and was held for ransom. He did not regain his freedom until 1158. The repercussions of Eskil's imprisonment could only put further strain upon the already unhappy relationship between the pope and the emperor.

Pope Adrian died unexpectedly in 1159 and the cardinal electors proved then to be divided between those who supported the emperor and those who opposed him. The papal throne passed to Alexander III who was unwilling to compromise with Barbarossa. The opposing faction duly crowned a pro-emperor candidate of their own - the anti-pope Victor IV. This created a schism between Church and emperor which was to endure for eighteen years.

Valdemar was now in an unfortunate position. In order not to invoke Barbarossa's anger, Valdemar was forced as the emperor's vassal to accept his anti-pope. Eskil, of course, could do no other than side with Rome's candidate. Both archbishop and king, against their wishes, were thus locked by politics into an impossible situation. Eskil tactfully left on a pilgrimage to Jerusalem, where we may assume that he renewed his acquaintance with Bertrand de Blanchefort, who was presiding as Grand Master of the Knights Templar. Instead of returning home Eskil then went into self-imposed exile. The place which he chose for his retreat was Clairvaux. His years there were to see Eskil deeply involved in a sequence of extremely momentous events. There can be little doubt that he was furthering the plans he had helped to devise with his late friend Bernard. The schism between the pope and the emperor made Clairvaux a prime centre of thought, philosophy and - not least in significance - of planning for the future. During these few years, the Knights Templar, free from any allegiance to kings or emperors, represented Rome's best defence. Eskil was inevitably part of the planning and decisions being made at Clairvaux. It is certain that, at Bernard's Clairvaux, he had a part to play, forming influential friendships and furthering the interests of his home state of Denmark.

This was a period when many important church leaders sought refuge in France. Thomas à Becket, Archbishop of Canterbury, did so in protest against Henry II's attack on the freedom and independence of the church in England. John of

Salisbury, the English theologian, came to study under St Bernard. Even Pope Alexander III was forced into temporary French exile in 1162.

It was at this time that Eskil must have laid his plans, in co-operation with the Chapters-General of the Cistercians and the Templars, for military operations against the pagans of Estonia.[16] There was an obvious reason for this action. European Christianity was growing in economic power. Trade in the Baltic was expanding rapidly and was, indeed, soon to lead to one of the strongest of commercial federations: the Hanseatic League. The north-eastern corner of the Baltic Sea was a gateway for traffic between Scandinavia and the Mediterranean. For centuries, the rivers of Russia had been important highways for trade between the north and the south of Europe. The gateway to which these highways led was becoming more and more commercially important. But, between Christian Russia and the Baltic gateway, lay the pagan land which is today Estonia, Latvia and Lithuania. For political, as well as for commercial stability, it was necessary to bring this area under Christian control.

These were the strategic considerations which occupied the Templars and the Cistercians and must, inevitably, have been of predominant importance to the plans for future policy which were being laid at Clairvaux. The military planning was made in accord with the Pope, Alexander III. Eskil met him in France on at least one occasion, in 1164. Details of their conference are lacking, but enough facts are available to create a coherent picture. Most obvious was the establishment in 1164 of an Estonian bishopric. At the time, there were no Christian communities in the country. Even so, a Cistercian monk, named Fulco from the northern French monastery of La Celle, was appointed bishop of Estonia. He was ordered by Pope Alexander to act under Eskil. This decision was a significant one, as Estonia was thereby established as part of the Danish sphere of influence. The northernmost of the Cistercian monasteries, Roma, was also founded in 1164 on the island of Gothland, the closest Christian community to Estonia.[17]

It was at this point that the situation in Denmark changed. Victor IV, the emperor's anti-pope, died in this same year, 1164. Continuing his disregard for Rome, the emperor again appointed his own pope, Paschal III. This, however, was more than King Valdemar could accept. He was anxious to heal the rift with his archbishop and refused to accept the second anti-pope. At last, in 1168, Eskil was able to return home to his archbishopric of Lund. Everything was now in place for the Church and the king to embark upon their planned mission against the pagans of Estonia. As a sign of the Church's goodwill toward Valdemar, Eskil and the Pope agreed to the canonisation of the king's murdered father, Knud Lavard.

[16] See Friedrich Benninghoven, *op cit.*
[17] *Ibid.*

Politically, this was an important decision, as it established the right of succession to the direct descendants of the new saint. It created what could be looked upon as a sort of divine right to the throne. Knud Lavard was canonised in a Papal Bull of 8 November 1169. This was celebrated in a magnificent ceremony on Midsummer Day of the following year, when Valdemar's eldest son, Knud, was created co-regent and heir to the throne by Archbishop Eskil.

CRUSADE

Preparations were now put in train for the joint military action against the pagan inhabitants of Estonia. A prime element in this strategy, which must have been part of the Clairvaux planning, was the pope's agreement that the warfare against the Baltic heathen was to be considered as a genuine crusade. This was a powerful attraction to the mediaeval Christian mind. For those who joined this crusade - as for those who made pilgrimage to the Holy Sepulchre in Jerusalem - a year of absolution was granted. For any who might be killed in combat, there was total absolution for all the sins committed during his lifetime.

Once the campaign in the Baltic gained the status of crusade, it was possible to augment the Danish force, and not simply with knights seeking remission for their sins. More important was the possibility of recruiting the already formidable military Order of Knights Templar. This, then, was the plan to which the Pope had agreed at Clairvaux in 1164. This was the cornerstone which made the procedure so ingenious a strategy. It can hardly be doubted that Eskil must have discussed such a possibility with the Templar Grand Master, Bertrand de Blanchefort, when on his pilgrimage to Jerusalem a few years earlier.

The campaign was finally precipitated by an Estonian raid launched from the island of Øsel (presently Saaremaa) upon Øland. This was seized as a convenient pretext and, on 11 September 1171, Pope Alexander at last proclaimed his long-promised crusade. To assuage 'the great bitterness and pain' felt by the pope in face of the savage depredations of the pagan Estonians, he demanded that the faithful should take up arms. There were to be many similar proclamations in the years to come, creating a state of virtually permanent warfare around the Baltic and eventually directly involving the Knights Templar.

Eskil was by now well into his seventies and feeling the weight of his years. With the crusade launched, he returned to Clairvaux, where he stayed until 1176. In the following year, the pope granted him permission to resign his office, with the right to appoint his own successor. In 1177, in a great ceremony at Lund Cathedral, in the king's presence, he laid the insignia of his archbishopric upon the altar, whence they were taken up by his relative, Absalon, the bishop of Roskilde. Eskil then retired to Clairvaux where, as a simple Cistercian, he lived out his final days.

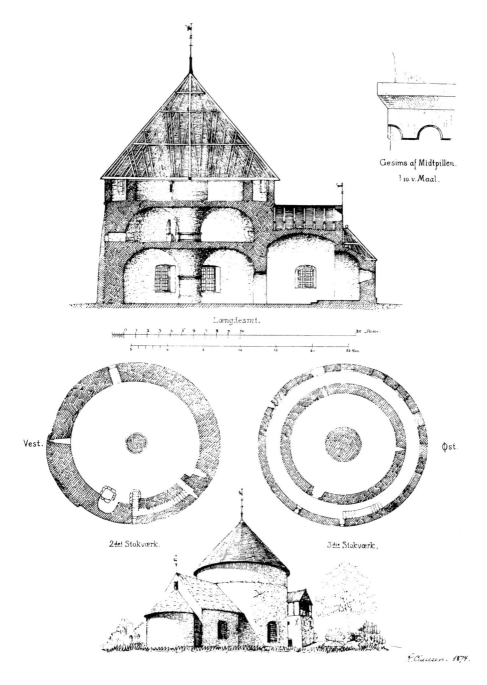

Gesims af Midtpillen.
$\frac{1}{10}$ v. Maal.

Længdesnit.

Vest.

Øst.

2det Stokværk.

3die Stokværk.

F. Claussen. 1874.

Nylars church

But the plans he had laid there, in concert with his friend Bernard, were now well in train. He died at Clairvaux in September 1181.

It is uncertain how many campaigns were launched between the first planning of the Danish Crusade against Estonia and the final conquest. But, since the plan seems already to have been laid in 1164 and there were frequent sorties over a period of 35 years, until the final battle in 1219, there must inevitably have been strategic operations on the islands which were placed conveniently along the route of the battle fleets. Now at last we are contemplating the fundamental basis of what led to the strange design and layout of the churches of Bornholm.

The massive interior structure of Bodilsker church.

There are, in fact, two other islands lying along the route of the crusading armies: Øland and Gothland. (See map p 32) The curious architecture, in particular the romanesque western towers of the Bornholm churches, finds an echo on Øland, and Gothland. It is also to be found in a very few churches on the mainland coast immediately adjacent to Øland, where there is a narrow strait which was convenient for the assembling of the fleets before their final leg across the Baltic. Nowhere else in Denmark is this church design to be found - a hint that their construction is associated with the crusading activity of the period.[18]

Although the exact date of the construction of the churches is uncertain, there now seems no doubt about their purpose. They were fortified structures which served as churches, watch-towers and store-houses for the provisioning of the crusader fleets. They may date from as early as 1164, (when the Cistercian Monastery at Roma in Gothland was built), or as late as 1219, when the final battle of the crusade was fought. The churches present one obvious hint as to their construction. Their ingenious combination of the ecclesiastical and the secular bears the unmistakable stamp of the Knights Templar. Not only do the round churches mirror their architectural style, their entire concept is redolent of Templar thinking. And there is no doubt of the Order's involvement in the final conquest of Estonia in 1219.

The Templars seem to have been established in Riga in 1202, with the name *Fratres Milicia Christi de Livonia* and became known as the Brothers of the Sword, a reference to their crimson device - a Cross upon a Sword. The first northern establishment of these Knights of Christ was created by a Cistercian, Theoderik von Treiden, who, like Fulco before him, became Bishop of Estonia.[19] Although the establishment was made in accord with the General Chapter of the Knights at Clairvaux, there was already the glimpse of an approaching schism between the pope and the powerful Order. While the General Chapter held the right to appoint its own master, the pope's permission for the foundation of the Riga Templars was conditional upon it being an independent command. The Order at Riga adhered to the so-called 'younger' Templar Rule, which had superseded the old Rule established in Troyes in 1128.[20] And the link with the Cistercians was ever present: Cistercian monasteries held copies of the Templar Rule. One must remember that, by now, Bernard of Clairvaux, the Templars' powerful protector, was long dead. But his hand can still be sensed in the working-out of the plans laid so many years before.

We may, therefore, infer from the record of the historical and political situation in the Baltic at this period, that the Order of Knights Templar brought their special

---

[18] Øland and Gothland are now Swedish. For refs to churches see *Hvem forsvarede hvad?* by Marit Angler in META 1984, nos 3-4. (META is a publication of the Mediaeval & Archaeological Society of Lund.)
[19] See Friedrich Benninghoven, *op cit.*
[20] K. Körner, *Die Templerregel*, Jena 1902.

expertise - as well as their fighting skills - to Bornholm. Much more important is their involvement in the construction of the island's churches which show clear evidence of the Templars' architectural style and which were built to serve the practical purpose of supply depots for the crusading fleets.

But the curiosity of the churches' style and purpose is not the most strange aspect of this puzzle. Their manner of construction does not explain why they were not more conveniently sited along the shore-line, where they would have been more immediately accessible for the loading and unloading of cargo. Some other motive must have dictated their emplacement. It is, of course, possible to make the easy assumption that the churches were simply placed to serve best the needs of the island's scattered population. But this will prove not to be the case. Another and more startling reason underlies the positioning of each church. There was a subtle, ingenious and hidden imperative which controlled the choice of the location for each building. And it was this curiosity of placing which opened the doorway into a profound and hidden page in the history of Bornholm.

Chapter Four

THE INVISIBLE PATTERN

The island of Bornholm covers an area of roughly 600 square kilometres, (230 square miles). It is a carefully chosen location where a treasure has been hidden, and that treasure is now the subject of our search. But this is not a treasure of gold and jewels, it is something much more precious. It is a treasure which the people who hid it considered to be beyond price. They have carefully preserved it, so that those who come after them may reap the harvest of their toil, and that harvest is the sum of centuries of labour and learning. It is – among many other things – a teaching aid. We, who unravel their message, will have much to learn, and the way into this treasure house of knowledge is through number and pattern.

The churches of Bornholm are locked together in an intricate geometric design, which can only be revealed when the key that unlocks them is detected - and used. That key must now be found and recognised. The church layout will suggest what seem to be straightforward patterns of what has come to be recognised as sacred geometry. It will also emphasise unusual and unsuspected relationships which are of great beauty. For the mathematician, there will prove to be a harmony which is akin to that created by a great composer, as he plays with the subtle sounds produced by a symphony orchestra. However, it is not necessary for the reader to be a mathematician in order to appreciate the elegance of the patterns, any more than it is necessary to understand the science of harmonics in order to enjoy great music. It is enough to be aware ... to listen to the cadences ... to see the patterns.

(Those readers who have the necessary mathematical expertise and who wish for the detailed calculations which lead to these conclusions, will find them later in this book, in Chapter 11.)

It seems best to begin the exploration of the ancient wonder by following the pathway of our original discovery, stripping layer after layer from the secrets veiled by the apparently random positioning of Bornholm's strange churches. On the island's 230 square mile area are a total of fifteen twelfth-century churches, twelve of which are the structures to be examined in this investigation.

Of these twelve churches, four are circular. The ground plan of each of the round churches shows them to be constructed in three circles. This circular shape is, in itself, interesting. Within the symbolism of sacred geometry, the circle is traditionally associated with the divine. Three circles are an expression of the three divine principles - in Christianity, the Father, the Son and the Holy Spirit. The number four, on the other hand, is an expression of Earth - the material world - the four corners of the universe - the four elements. As we have already noted in Chapter Two, the square - or the cross - within the circle is a representation of both these ideas. It is a combination of the divine and the material, among the oldest and most profound of all the elements of geometric symbolism.

Figure 1

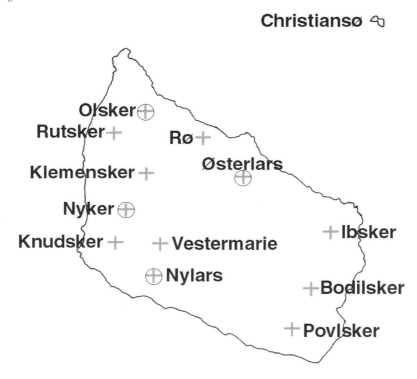

On Bornholm, we have four round churches on an island which is itself a tolerably regular quadrilateral. There need, of course, be no significance whatever in this simple fact. However, that just four churches of circular shape have been built upon a four-sided island is worthy of note, given the significance once attached to the number, allied as it is with the three-level structure of the buildings, which in its turn suggests a relationship with the Trinity.

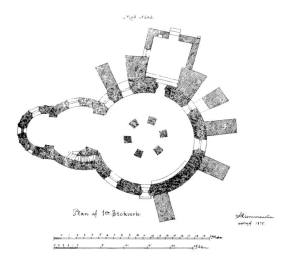

Ground plan of Østerlars church. Three interlinked circles. The church is dedicated to St Laurence [Lars]. The name means 'Eastern Laurence'. This suggests the presence of a 'Western Laurence' – but no such church exists on Bornholm. However, the main church of the original diocese of Lund is also dedicated to St Laurence, which may account for the oddity.

Could there be a geometric pattern in their placing? It was just this simple question which came to mind and which triggered this investigation long before we had any knowledge of the Baltic Crusades, or the presence of the Knights Templar in this remote corner of the Christian world.

But a first glance at the positioning of the churches is disappointing.

Figure 2

They are certainly not on a straight line. Neither are they on the circumference of a circle. Nor does their layout seem to suggest any other recognisable pattern.[21] However, a closer examination reveals a simple geometric configuration. The line connecting the two easternmost churches intersects the line between the western pair at an angle which seems to be very close to thirty degrees.

Figure 3

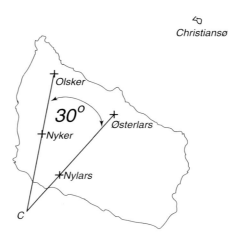

This 30° angle is geometrically simple to construct. It is almost as simple as the drawing of a straight line, or a circle. It is, moreover, common in sacred geometry, as it is part of the formation of the very well-known six-pointed Star of David. To find such an interesting angle in the intersecting lines of the churches could, of course be no more than coincidence. In order, therefore, to establish whether the ground beneath our feet can lay claim to any stability, we must first consider the important matter of accuracy.

If the angle, when drawn upon a map, is not exactly thirty degrees but appears to be, say, twenty-eight or thirty-one degrees, it would still be difficult to be sure that we are not drifting into uncertainty. And this is compounded by the further problem that we cannot know to what level of accuracy the original constructors, (if such there were), were working.

[21] The observation has been made that the layout bears a resemblance to that of the constellation Corvus – the Raven. While this may be interesting, it is nonetheless moving into the subjective area of interpretation. A brief exploration of the ideas raised by this hypothesis will be found in the Appendix.

From our present standpoint in the investigation, we cannot assume that our ancestors were even capable of the feat of measuring accurate angles over large distances. Consequently, if any claim is to be made for the precision of the work, then the degree of accuracy must be defined within very strict limits. With proof of absolute accuracy, it will be possible to argue for intention. Without it, nothing can be either proved or disproved. However, if such proofs should indeed be forthcoming, then we would certainly have grounds to adjust our impressions of the capabilities of the designers of the layout.

It is, perhaps, not surprising that no serious scientific research has yet been undertaken which might help to shed light on this possibility. The required parameters appear vague and unscientific. They also seem dependent upon each other, while remaining, for the most part, difficult to determine. However, despite the common opinion to the contrary, the parameters are not all unknown. It is beyond dispute that our ancestors possessed remarkable skills in the construction of complex geometrical patterns. Nowhere, for example, in the building of the Great Pyramid, did the Egyptians stray by more than 0.1 per cent (1:1000) from geometric perfection.[22]

In Denmark itself there is extremely well documented evidence of such expertise. In 1948, Professor P.E. Nørlund of Copenhagen University, published the results of his work on the mysterious Danish construction known as Trelleborg. This is a circular, fortress-like structure which was built before 1000 AD. It is constructed with astonishing symmetry and in impeccable geometric patterns. Nørlund's measurements show that the layout is accurate to within one or two centimetres over a distance of several hundred metres and nowhere do the angles show any deviation greater than 0.2 of a degree.[23] How, or why, Trelleborg was built with such precision is not known.

While we can conclude from the forgoing that the builders were capable of highly sophisticated work in the laying out of advanced geometric configurations, the examples which historians have, thus far, investigated are all relatively small in dimension. The employment of such techniques over very long distances had not been noticed or reported until our publication of *The Holy Place* in 1991.

However, even though the construction of small designs of a few hundred yards may be easier to comprehend, there is no reason to conclude that the proficiency of the builders was limited to such small-scale undertakings. The techniques required are the same, whether the layout be 200 yards or 200 miles. The only additional requirement is the time needed to carry out the task, which remains

---

[22] Robert Poulson, *Den Store Pyramide*, Gyldendal, Copenhagen, 1980.
[23] P.E. Nørlund, *Trelleborg*, Copenhagen, 1948.

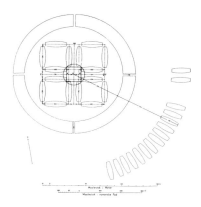

Trelleborg, the mysterious Viking settlement, built to a precise and measured geometry.

simply one of calculation and the precise measurement of angles. The problem can be reduced to the straightforward question: did they know how to do it? And the evidence clearly shows that they did.

We must now return to Bornholm to confront this basic problem. If the four round churches on the quadrilateral island were intended to be positioned in a precise geometrical relationship to one another, then what degree of accuracy may be expected in the layout? This question, as already indicated, is of prime importance. If the accuracy is not within very strict and narrow limits, it will be impossible to establish whether a given pattern is intended, or is merely the result of a lucky coincidence.

Thus far, we have identified an angle of 30°. But how precise is this measurement? Not surprisingly, it was originally identified by drawing lines upon the map (as in Fig 3), and measuring the angle with a simple protractor. This, however, cannot be expected to produce a very satisfactory result. With the appropriate pen, a line can be drawn which is as narrow as one tenth of a millimetre – a thin line, certainly. But, with a map scale of 1:50000, the line in the real landscape is fifty thousand times thicker, i.e. 5 metres. Any attempt to measure the angle formed by two intersecting lines is naturally blurred by the simple fact that the two lines are themselves covering 10 metres of ground surface, not to mention the additional latitude produced by the thickness of the measuring scale inscribed upon the protractor. Using such crude methods, it will never be possible to be certain that the measurements are within the strict limits which the research demands.

There is yet another obvious problem. How accurate is the map? In the not too distant past, maps were based upon a laborious measuring of the landscape, from point to point, using precise surveying instruments, and the results were then carefully drawn by skilled draughtsmen. But, even with the meticulous care which was exercised in the preparation of the maps, mistakes could still occur. Indeed, in our own researches into the geometric system of Rennes-le-Château, we found that the cartographers of the French *Institut Géographique* had completely misplaced one of the churches, drawing it on the wrong side of its village square. It was both startling - and satisfying - to find that the accuracy of the geometric layout had unerringly indicated the cartographer's mistake.[24]

Modern maps are generally created from satellite photographs, in which such major errors are unlikely. Much more laborious methods were once necessary and only very few sites could be fixed with absolute precision. Convenient elements in the landscape were selected - i.e. hilltops or naturally pointed buildings such as church spires - which were designated as trigonometric points. The positions of these key 'trig' points were then surveyed with extreme care. Using the rules of geometry as applied to triangles, it was thus possible to calculate a distance by ascertaining the precise angle between a chosen position and any two of the known fixed trig points. But even with the more reliable maps of today, if an investigation is carried out, not on the ground, but upon a drawn representation, then uncertainties must remain. No matter how accurately produced the map may be, even the slightest stretching of the paper can compound an inaccuracy already inherent in the thickness of a drawn line.

By great good fortune, the Bornholm research was spared such problems. The fifteen mediaeval churches have all been chosen as trig points by the Danish official institute for map-production, the *Kort & Matrikelstyrelsen*. The exact co-ordinates of the crosses fixed upon the church towers have been meticulously calculated and are published in readily available tables. The relative positions of the churches have thus been pin-pointed to the accuracy of a millimetre and it is therefore possible to calculate any distance or angle with absolute precision.

A brief explanatory note is here necessary: Bornholm's co-ordinate system is measured from the antenna on a tower close to the island's highest point which, fortuitously, lies in the middle of the land mass. Its co-ordinates have been designated as: $X = 50,000.00$, $Y = 50,000.00$. All other co-ordinates are measured from this point. The co-ordinate system is, of course, flat, while the surface of the earth is spherical. However, since the entire system covers a square of no more than 50 x 50 kilometres, adjustments from the flat to the spherical will have no significant effect upon the measurements. This point is made, as it is essential that the reader should understand that these basic considerations have been an integral part of this investigation.[25]

[24] See *The Holy Place.* p148.
[25] The official co-ordinates of the churches are listed on p 177.

The four round churches of Bornholm are Østerlars, Nylars, Olsker and Nyker. Using the official co-ordinates supplied for these churches, the two lines shown in Figure 3 are found to intersect at an angle of precisely 30.18° - measured from cross to cross - that is from centre to centre - of the circular buildings. Thus it is

The round churches of Olsker (left) and Nyker (right). Nyker means 'New Church' – its original dedication was to All Saints. Unlike the other round churches, which are built on three levels, Nyker has only two. There is a staircase leading to the non-existent upper level, which suggests that the original third floor was dismantled – or, perhaps, never constructed.

established that the angle is not 29° - nor is it 31°. The angle is certainly 30° with a deviation of less than 0.2°. For those readers who are unused to thinking in such terms, and for whom the idea of 0.2° carries little clear visual meaning, we make the following suggestion. Hold out a matchstick at arm's length and look towards a distant horizon. Very little of that horizon will be blocked out by the two millimetre width of the match. But this is *more* than 0.2°. All the geometry of the Bornholm system is more accurate than this.

Another visual aid would be to consider the minute divisions on a large clock face. If the clock were to be showing not the sixty minutes of an hour but the 360 degrees of a circle, then each of those sixty divisions would be divided into six further parts. To show 0.2°, each of these tiny sections would have to be yet further divided into 5 more parts. The clock face would now be showing eighteen hundred equal divisions, each measuring 0.2°. The Bornholm system betters this degree of precision. It is to be doubted that such accuracy could possibly be defined by the use of drawn lines upon a map printed on paper.

Having found one example of such exactitude, we should now expect to find at least a similar level of accuracy throughout the entire system - if, that is, the construction is to be seen as demonstrating intent and not merely the haphazard working of coincidence.

EXTENDED SEARCH

Thus far, an angle of thirty degrees has been identified, laid out with a sufficient measure of accuracy to suggest a possible geometric design. But the four round churches, even with their interesting angle, do not appear to be creating a pattern of any kind. And yet, their placing is presenting us with a geometric key. Once deciphered, this key will be seen to be controlling the positioning of Bornholm's mediaeval churches in an astonishing and sophisticated way. But how is it to be deciphered? The approach must be systematic: the search is for a pattern which can be termed 'sacred geometry'. The pattern must, moreover, demonstrate an acceptable level of accuracy - i.e. to within 0.2° or better.

Patterns in sacred geometry can be seen, in general, to be symmetrical. The pattern we are seeking should, therefore, have an axis - as the vertical line through a nose defines the axis of a symmetrical face. And there must be a clearly defined central point. If the four round churches are, indeed, part of a sacred pattern, then one of them should be identifiable as the centre.

The massive walls of Østerlars.

Of the four round churches, Østerlars is the largest and most impressive. As with all the churches of Bornholm, it is a beautifully maintained and handsome structure. Its massive walls are regularly repainted so that it gleams a dazzling white against the sky. The interior is a place of calm, space and light, the huge, round, central supporting pillar bringing a splash of colour with its wonderful and lively mediaeval painted decoration, including a spectacular devil figure presiding over a crowd of the tortured damned.

Østerlars lays a clear claim to be the logical place to begin a search for the heart of the design. And as the central point, with the distance between Østerlars and Nylars fixing the radius, a circle produces an interesting result:

Figure 4

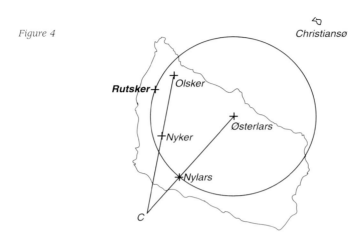

The church of Rutsker lies upon the circumference of the circle. Østerlars is therefore equidistant from both Nylars and Rutsker. But imprecision is inevitable when working with drawn lines upon a map and we could, again, be confronting a coincidence. The official table of co-ordinates, however, enables us to check the distances.

The co-ordinates show that the distance from Østerlars to Nylars is 14,335.585 metres. From Østerlars to Rutsker : 14,335.71.[26] With the precision available using modern techniques, the distance between the crosses on the spires proves to vary by no more than twelve centimetres. (This is a little less than four and three quarter inches over a measured distance of just under nine miles.) It should be borne in mind, moreover, that the exact spot on the church cross which has been chosen to fix the measurement is one selected by the surveyors of the Danish official mapping institute. It was not chosen in order to demonstrate the equidistance of the structures. The span, however, appears to be very close to 14336 metres. When, later, the units of measure are examined, this number will prove to be considerably more important - and significant - than it presently appears.

The result, so far, enables us to state with confidence that the churches of Nylars and Rutsker are, beyond argument, equidistant from the centre of Østerlars church. We appear to be confronting 'intention'. If so, then we have identified a

---

[26] The calculations are to be found in Chapter 11.

basic component of the pattern: Østerlars is a centre - Østerlars / Nylars the axis and radius.

Circle, centre and axis provide, in geometric terms, the necessary elements to define and orientate the system. The orientation is important. With nothing but a circle and a centre, it would be possible to construct any number of internal 'sacred' geometrical figures. But, with the orientation - the main axis - defined, in this case by the Østerlars / Nylars line, the possibilities immediately become limited.

For example, the most familiar of all sacred patterns is the six-pointed Star of David. With the orientation fixed, there is only one six-pointed star which can be inscribed within the circle.

Figure 5

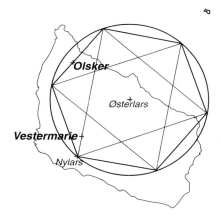

And on the face of the star's enclosing hexagon we find Olsker - one of our original key round churches. Coincidence yet again? Had Olsker been placed with precision upon one of the star points, the likelihood of chance would have been much diminished. But there is no such obvious intent. More evidence is necessary in order to strengthen the argument against 'blind fortune'. If we are truly uncovering a systematic purpose, then the placing of Olsker Church should be demonstrating a simple geometric relationship. And indeed, for a mathematician, the placing is of specific beauty. It reveals proportions which are extraordinarily harmonious.

It is now possible to see (Figure 6, page 52) that the very first of the drawn lines which indicated the thirty degree angle in the church alignments, are locked with exactitude to a much more complex geometrical pattern. The lines provide both orientation and radius of a circle. They also mark the intersections of its internal square and hexagon, with Olsker defining the distance to the hexagon's face. This intricate, yet simply produced pattern is the key. It contains all the geometric relationships which are needed, to create and control the total layout of the

Figure 6

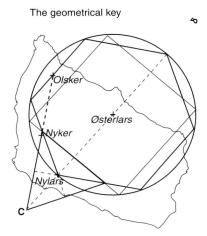

The geometrical key

Bornholm design. The first confirmation of this astonishing and ingenious enterprise is to be found when the internal hexagon - the six-sided figure - is examined.

As can be seen in Figure 5 on page 51, it proves to include, on a chord of the hexagon, yet another of the mediaeval churches - Vestermarie. This is so placed that its distance from the point of the star (Nylars) appears to be equal to a quarter of the circle's radius, i.e. it is one fourth of the distance from Nylars to Østerlars. Again, it is necessary to confirm the degree of accuracy in the placing.

Here, we are presented with what appears to be a problem. Vestermarie is not a round church. The measurement, therefore, has no obvious 'target', such as is provided by the centre of a circle. And this time, there is a lack of precision. This time, the measure from trig point to trig point, (from church cross to church cross), is not accurate to within a few inches, but only to an approximate twenty or so metres. Nor, as Figure 7 shows, does the theoretical mathematically indicated spot even lie within the church building.

Figure 7

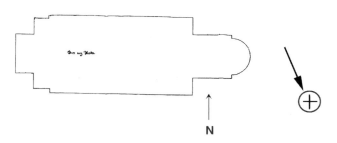

N

Figure, stamped from sheet gold (actual size less than an inch high) and depicting a long-haired regal figure. More than three thousand have been unearthed on Bornholm since 1985. There are more than a hundred different patterns, of which this is the most common. Their purpose and function remain enigmatic.

Østerlars Church. The conical roof is a late addition. It covers the original flat roof from which rose a rotunda, formed by the hollow central pillar.

The slit windows in the rotunda were carefully aligned upon the midsummer and midwinter sunrise. The solstice sunrise pierces the rotunda of Østerlars church.

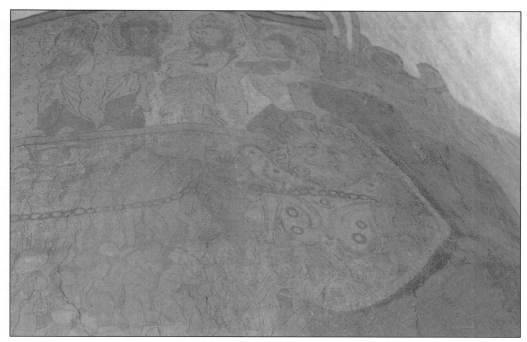

The fearsome devil fresco on Østerlars' central pillar.

The massive arcaded central pillar of Østerlars church.

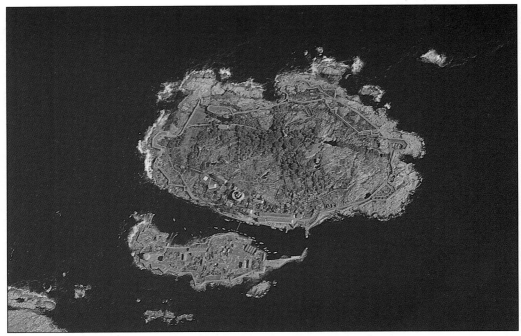

The tiny islet of Christiansø, some twelve and a half miles to the north-east of Bornholm.
It lies on the main axis of the layout and contributes with precision to the geometric design.

Cross in Nylars church – perhaps an echo of the Knights Templar.

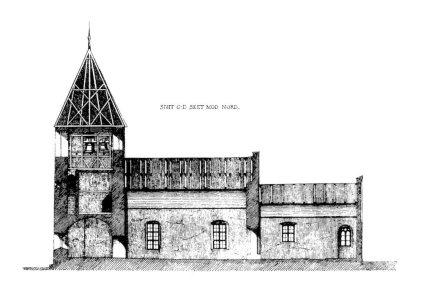

SNIT C-D SEET MOD NORD.

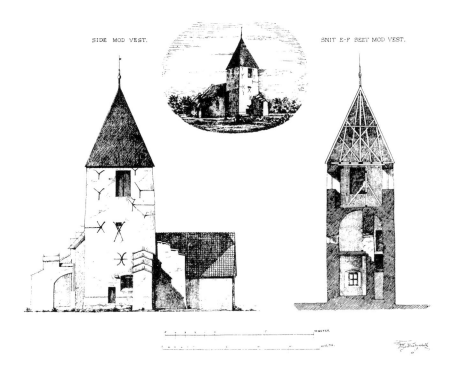

SIDE MOD VEST.

SNIT E-F SEET MOD VEST.

Vestermarie's original church, demolished at the end of the nineteenth century.

When this discrepancy was first noted, we were confronted by several possibilities. We might have been encountering a looseness in the design, implying that its creators could only work to a rough degree of exactitude. (In which case, it would never be possible to be certain that any measurement was intended.) Or they had made a mistake. Or we were completely wrong - and the design was no more than the result of our fevered imaginations. In the event, the inaccuracy shown by the co-ordinates of Vestermarie Church proved to be nothing of the kind. In fact, it provided unexpected and convincing confirmation of the intent that is inherent in the design which we were uncovering. Vestermarie Church is not the original mediaeval construction.

The 1880s were an unfortunate time for the old churches of Bornholm. Rø, Klemensker and Vestermarie were all torn down and rebuilt within the decade. We had, at first, assumed that the new churches stood exactly on the foundations of their predecessors and our original calculations were therefore based on the official co-ordinates provided by the *Kort & Matrikelstyrelsen*. They showed, however, that the present building appeared to be 21 metres north west of the theoretical point indicated by the measurements.

The present Vestermarie, photographed from the exact position of the altar of the original church.

Fortunately, the architect's drawings for the new construction have survived. In one of these, he shows the position and orientation of the new church as it is placed in relation to the original structure.

Figure 8

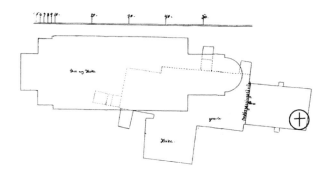

And it is clear that the old church was differently positioned and oriented. Its axis was turned a few degrees from the true east-west line. But when plotted from the plan and the official co-ordinates, the mathematically indicated spot proved to be placed *exactly* upon the altar of the original church. Such precision can only be construed as the strongest of possible evidence for our looked-for intent. And it was now indicated that, for those churches which were not circular, the key placing should lie in what is, after all, the obvious spot – the holy altar.

OLSKER

The question of the accuracy of the placing of Olsker Church has not yet been addressed. This, too, will be found to contain details of extreme interest. In addition, it will add yet more to the demonstration of the carefully prepared plan which was being put into operation.

Thus far, the layout has proved to be better than the target accuracy of 0.2 of a degree. Other positions examined have demonstrated 100 per cent exactitude. In fact, the only noticeable aberration has been the original 0.2° associated with the first thirty degree angle - which was itself defined by the Olsker / Nyker line. If the accuracy is, indeed, to prove better than the target set, then this anomalous tiny discrepancy merits attention.

With the awareness of a possible underlying pattern, the detailed examination of the position of Olsker Church, in relation to its theoretical position, shows a totally unexpected discrepancy. Olsker is found to be a full sixty-two metres due east of its apparently intended site. So large an apparent inaccuracy does not arise anywhere else in the investigation and appears, therefore, to present a well-nigh insuperable problem in the proving of the geometric system.[27] But chance can sometimes be a powerful ally.

By great good fortune, in a field adjacent to Olsker church, a hoard of silver treasure has recently (1993) been found and Bornholm's museum accordingly organised an archaeological investigation. Aerial photographs were taken and it was reported that an underground structure had been identified close to the church. Expert opinion considered this to be the foundations of a building which was in existence at the time of the erection of the church. The press reports, however, did not specify the exact location of the find. We accordingly contacted Finn Ole Sonne Nielsen, the archaeologist concerned, and asked if this trace of foundations could possibly lie sixty-two metres due east of the present church? This, he told us, was exactly what the aerial photographs showed.

[27] The 'intended site' is the altar, twelve metres east of the actual co-ordinates given in the table on p.177.

It would seem that at the time when the building of the church was planned, there was already a structure in existence at the designated spot. This must, then, be presumed to have been of considerable importance; sufficiently so, in order to preclude its demolition and the accurate positioning of the church. At the moment of writing, no excavations have yet been carried out. We await - with interest - the archaeologists' findings.

Already we can make the confident statement that suspicion has become certainty. Discovery has followed upon discovery, each bringing additional confirmation that the church pattern of Bornholm cannot be attributed to coincidence.

A beautifully harmonious pattern has been revealed, fixed, thus far, by six of Bornholm's mediaeval churches and clearly showing the intent for which we have been seeking. But there remain yet more churches on the island to be investigated. We have insisted on a deviation of no more than 0.2° in order acceptably to prove that intent. The remainder of this investigation will show that the accuracy of the design is better than this. In most cases, the system will prove to show no measurable deviation of any kind.

The absolute proofs of this statement will, of necessity, require detailed mathematical demonstration. We are aware that, for the majority of our readers, such proofs lie in a daunting and rarified area, requiring an expertise which is far beyond what most of us will remember from our schooldays. Yet worse . . . they make for very difficult and dry reading. But they cannot be avoided. We have accordingly reserved them for the last chapter of this book. The immediately following pages, therefore, present no more than the easily understood surface layers of the design. These are the elements which can be simply visualised and which convey the readily comprehensible geometric facts. In these patterns can be found the knowledge which the designers wished to preserve and to pass on to us - their heirs.

Chapter Five

STAR PATTERNS

The geometry which we are exploring reflects a way of thinking which is far from anything which might be termed conventional. In addition, it also demonstrates a capacity for measuring large distances with an extreme accuracy. The opinion of modern historians seems to be that such skills were not within the capabilities of the society which was responsible for the Bornholm layout.

But, as already noted, evidence of similar astonishingly complex mathematical and geometrical methods is clearly to be found. It is present, for example, in the building of the Gothic cathedrals which date from the same period. In his book on Chartres Cathedral, Louis Charpentier analyses the geometrical proportions of the building. In particular, he identifies the major role played by the seven-pointed star - the heptagon - in the cathedral's ground plan.[28]

Figure 9

[28] Louis Charpentier, *Les mystères de la cathédrale de Chartres*, Laffont 1966.

We shall find that even such complex figures as this find their reflection in the landscape of Bornholm, as do other meaningful geometric forms.

The design which we have termed 'the geometric key' is illustrated in Figure 6 on p 52. It shows with what subtlety the four round churches have been placed in order to indicate the position and orientation of the circle, as well as its inscribed square, even though none of them is set upon the latter figure's circumference. The indicator lies solely in the logic of the geometry. The symbolic importance of the square within the circle has already been discussed in Chapter Two, but this deceptively simple device merits further consideration.

For example, the pattern can be infinitely reproduced. Circles can be inscribed within squares within circles *ad infinitum*. The same process can of course be pursued outwards - with squares enclosed by circles enclosed by squares - until the universe is filled with the three basic and incommensurate proportions.

Figure 6 above shows the square inscribed within the circle. The inevitable next step is to inscribe a circle within the square. And again, the new circumference intersects yet another church. Klemensker Church is placed upon the inner circle with the same degree of exactitude that is displayed by Rutsker church upon the outer (see Figure 4).

Figure 10

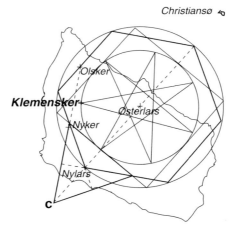

Christiansø

And with Klemensker we are taken into the very soul of the gothic cathedral. As the above diagram shows, the distance from Klemensker church to the intersection with the main axis of the design, (the Østerlars/Nylars line), is one seventh of the circle's circumference. The church is placed upon the tip of a seven-pointed star.

The placing is impressively accurate - though not precise. While the church lies exactly upon the circumference of the circle, the heptagon's point lies six metres to the south of the church wall. (For exact calculations see Chapter 11) But again we are dealing with one of the nineteenth century reconstructions and not with the original mediaeval church. As with Vestermarie, one is bound to ask if the new structure has been placed exactly upon the foundations of the old, but in this case it has not been possible to find confirmation of the fact. The geometry implies, however, that as with Vestermarie, the building has been shifted by a tiny distance.

Consider again the above Figure 10. It shows a circle with its contained square and inner circle - and holding a triangle, a square, a hexagon and a heptagon in harmonious relationship, oriented and fixed by the layout of the churches.

The mathematically informed reader will appreciate the special skill employed in the layout of the seven-pointed star. The three-, four- and six-sided figures can all be simply drawn by the use of a ruler and a pair of compasses. But the heptagon is impossible to construct by such simple and straightforward geometrical means. Further exploration of this beautiful design will be found in Chapter 11. The system itself will demonstrate the manner in which the creation of the seven-pointed star was achieved.

SYMBOLISM

In Chapter Two, we have discussed the existence of the three number systems - the rational, irrational and transcendental numbers - which together describe the universe. These we must now reconsider, for the next step in Bornholm's geometry leads to a link between the numbers and their symbolic values.

It would seem that there is no coincidence in the fact that the church which divides the circle circumference by seven is dedicated to Saint Clement, (Klemensker means Clement's Church). He was one of the Fathers of the early Church and has left some interesting writings. In *Stromata*, his most important work, he discusses 'a higher knowledge' contained within Christianity. The instructed Christian, he says, is 'the true Gnostic ... the perfect Christian', whose faith, he tells us, is related to Knowledge.

In Hermetic thought, rational numbers symbolise our 'rational' - material - world. Irrational numbers symbolise the world of dreams, thoughts, ideas - the immaterial or spiritual world. The heptagon indicated by Klemensker church is a clear reference to the number seven, the traditional symbol of wisdom. Seven is a rational number, its irrational equivalent is square-root seven ($\sqrt{7}$), which symbolises spiritual wisdom. And this is the aspect indicated by the positioning of yet another of Bornholm's churches, Ibsker, which is Jacob's (James's) church.

The distance between Østerlars and Nylars is the controlling length of the Bornholm System. Calculations reveal that this distance is in a very precise relationship with the distance between the other two round churches, Olsker and Nyker. The link is found to be square root seven, in the following manner. If the distance from Olsker to Nyker is used to define the radius of another circle centred upon Østerlars, then the church of Ibsker lies upon its circumference.

Figure 11

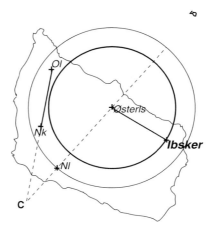

This same radius is now doubled and an equilateral triangle, with faces tangent to the inner circle is inscribed. With one hundred percent accuracy, each face of that triangle proves to be equal to the basic Østerlars / Nylars radius multiplied by the square root of seven.

Figure 12

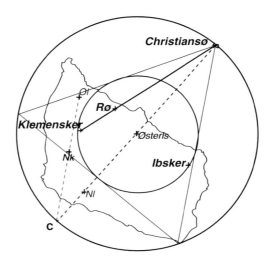

St Olav, the Norwegian King, to whom the church is dedicated, above the porch of Olsker.

The concept of spiritual wisdom, allied with the Trinity, is recorded in the square-root seven triangle whose dimensions are fixed by the placing of the round churches. It is Ibsker church which lies on the defining circle. St James makes his appropriate, and significant, contribution.

Now the Bornholm mystery shifts into yet another dimension. This new outer circle produces an unlooked-for, and in some senses disturbing, fact. We describe this fact as 'disturbing', because it falls into that category of discovery which we were once advised by a Cambridge academic not to report. The reason for his caution was simply the difficulty of explaining something which seems so unlikely that it has to be labelled 'impossible'. It seems to us, however, that to suppress difficult information is no more than cowardice. Our task is to report what we have discovered, however unlikely it may seem. Facts are not negated simply because they are uncomfortable. The cry that it cannot be has little force against the simple statement that it is.

In order fully to grasp the significance of this new aspect of the discovery, it is necessary to make a brief digression into the geology of the island of Bornholm which is, in itself, unusual.

CHRISTIANSØ

Geologically speaking, Bornholm is among the more interesting locations on the surface of the earth. Essentially a massive piece of Precambrian granite, the island is one of the oldest portions of the visible surface of our world. It is a huge rock, created through volcanic activity some 1700 million years ago. In its origins, it was the base of an enormous mountain well over six miles high which, over the millions of years has eroded to this 225 square mile island, which was left behind when the surrounding land surface sank and the Baltic Sea was created.

Apart from Bornholm itself, there is one other vestige of the great primordial mountain, which still rises above the surface of the sea. This is the tiny islet of Christiansø, which lies about 20 kilometres, (twelve and a half miles), from the northern shore of Bornholm. This speck of land measures no more than seven hundred metres, (less than half a mile), on its longest side. As can be seen in Figure 12 above, it lies precisely at the apex of the square-root seven triangle. It is also exactly placed upon the prolongation of the central axis of the system.

One can sense the desire to claim that such precision of placing is nothing more than the fruit of random coincidence. And, indeed, what else can it be? Nevertheless, 'coincidence' has placed this fragment of rock in an astonishingly meaningful geometric relationship with the rest of the Bornholm system. The designers of the system must have been aware of this fact. They certainly took advantage of it. Two other of the mediaeval churches, Klemensker and Rø, are unerringly aligned upon this same point.

There is no evidence that Christiansø was inhabited at the time when the Bornholm churches were constructed. There is certainly no trace of a mediaeval church anywhere upon the island. Interestingly, though, long before the tiny scrap of land received its present name, it was known as Kirkholmen - Church Island.[29] The new name was adopted after 1684, when the Danish King Christian V established a military base to replace those lost when Denmark was forced to cede all land east of Copenhagen, (Bornholm excepted), to Sweden.

The fortress was in operation until the middle of the nineteenth century. It is now an unique historical monument, untouched since it was abandoned by the army and much frequented by summer tourists. But, in drawing this remote speck of land into Bornholm's geometric system, are we, truly, merely forcing a wishfully created design upon the haphazard alignments of nature? If we are, then we are certainly not the first to recognise the wonder.

At the exact spot on Christiansø where the circle meets the apex of the triangle, there was once a rock carving which seems to have been carefully placed to indicate this important intersection of the geometry. The carving took the form of a great compass. Sadly, this precious indication vanished when the rocks were dynamited, to be used as building material in the construction of the fortress. There is, however, surviving documentary evidence for the existence of the carved compass.

The letter (opposite), presently in the Danish National Archive[30], was written in 1756 by Captain Herman Bohn Wolfsen, the Commanding Officer of the garrison

[29] Anker E. Kofoed, *Christiansøs Histoire*, Rønne, 1984.
[30] *Protocoll over …. Kongelige Expeditioner* - 1756

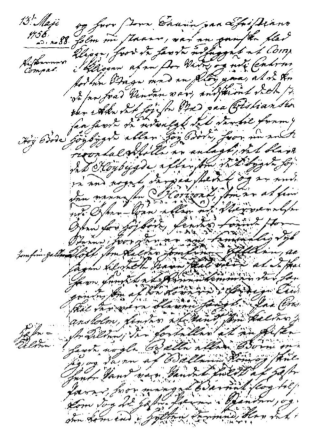

Fragment of the letter by Captain Wolfsen.
(Danish State Archive.)

on Christiansø. It was sent to one of his friends, Catering Inspector Birch of the Danish Admiralty. Captain Wolfsen writes at length concerning the conditions of life on the island and recounts what he has been able to learn 'from the old men who knew the place before it was taken over as a fortress.' He says:

> In blessed King Christian V's time, a fortress was built here and given the name of Christiansø. Previously it had been a base for the fishermen of Svanicke, Liste, Bøllshavn and Gudhjem as well as others from (the north of) Bornholm who made use of it. They had built huts there and where the *Store Tårn* (Great Tower) now stands, there was a completely flat rock, where they had carved an enormous compass, in the centre of which was a pole with a vane so that they could gauge the direction of the wind. Although this place was not the highest spot on Christiansø, they had chosen it rather than Høybygde or Høybode, where there is now a mill.

The Captain is clearly puzzled by the placing of the wind vane on the flat rock rather than on the high point of the island, which would, indeed, have been more practical. But the fishermen were in fact using a compass which had been carved at least four centuries earlier. It now seems that the purpose of the carving was not to measure the wind, but rather to mark the intersection of Bornholm's extraordinary geometry. Calculations show that the exact spot is a few metres outside the wall of the *Store Tårn* (see Chapter 11) It lies precisely where the rock shows clear evidence of having been blasted away at the time of the tower's construction.

We have mentioned above that the churches of Klemensker and Rø are also aligned upon the compass point. It is further interesting to note that the distance between these two churches is exactly one half of the system's main defining measurement: i.e. it is precisely equal to half the distance between Østerlars church and Nylars church.

THE FIVE-POINTED STAR

The basic measure and the disposition of the four round churches has enabled us to identify three-, four-, six- and seven-sided figures in the Bornholm layout. But what of that most significant star-shape, the Pentacle, which is still missing? The five-pointed star lies at the heart of this mystery. It was the first geometric shape to present itself in the earliest days of the Rennes-le-Château research and the discovery of the famous Pentacle of Mountains[31] was the signpost which indicated the path to be followed.

Nothing could be more certain than that Bornholm would reveal this most significant of figures. Professor Christopher Cornford, who discovered the pentagonal sub-structure of Nicolas Poussin's painting of *The Shepherds of Arcadia* pointed out that this shape 'enjoyed immense prestige and excited nothing short of reverence among geometers, architects and masons since very ancient times.' The five-pointed star is the symbol of what came to be known as the Divine Proportion - now, more commonly, the Golden Section or Golden Division.

The Golden Section is curious and fascinating. In the simplest of terms, it is the way of dividing a line so that the smaller part is in exact relation to the greater, as the greater part is to the whole. Thus in the diagram below, the line AC is divided at B in such a manner that AB is to BC as BC is to AC.

A   B   C

[31] See *The Holy Place*.

The proportion, expressed mathematically, is $(\sqrt{5}+1) : 2$ or, as a decimal fraction, 1 : 1.618... When used by a painter to divide a picture, the Golden Division produces a sense of harmony and balance. The viewer, even if unaware, responds to its presence. It conveys a feeling of 'rightness', and indeed it is to be found in the very workings of nature. The divine proportion determines the spiral shape of a snail's shell. It determines the positions of the seeds in a sunflower's head. The seemingly cold and mathematical juxtaposition of one unit against another of the greater length of 1.618 is, in some indefinable way, aesthetically pleasing to the human brain.

The ratio 1 : 1.618 has many intriguing properties. The well-known Fibonacci Series leads ever closer to it. This Series is made up of numbers which are equal to the sum of the two previous numbers in the list: 1 : 1 : 2 : 3 : 5 : 8 : 13 : 21 : 34 ..... and so on. The sequence provides a means of calculating proportions which approach the Golden Section. Any number divided by the one preceding will give an ever more accurate approximation. Five divided by three = 1.666; 8 ÷ 5 = 1.6 ; 13 ÷ 8 = 1.625; 21 ÷ 13 = 1.615 ... The greater the numbers, the closer comes the Golden Section.

A further curiosity lies in the square of the number. To multiply 1.618 by itself is the same as adding one : 1.618 x 1.618 = 2.618. Expressed in the abstract - algebraically - it seems (to the non-mathematician) bizarre : $x^2 = x + 1$. Also, to divide 1 by 1.618 is to subtract one : 1 ÷ 1.618 = 0.618.

The Golden Section was considered by the ancient mathematicians such as Pythagoras, to be the symbol of Life and Eternity. It was looked on as a magical number and it is embodied in the Five-Pointed Star - the Pentacle, - the shape used by magicians for conjuration.

Figure 13

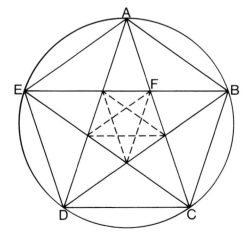

The lines which create the star divide themselves precisely in the proportion of 1 : 1.618. Where are we to find this powerful figure on Bornholm? Not surprisingly, it is hidden in a most ingenious way and it is the Golden Section which leads to it. In Figure 3 (page 44), the intersection point of the two lines which create the thirty degree angle has been labelled as Point C. The distance from Østerlars to Nylars has proved to be the controlling radius which has led to the star shapes. Now, it is the distance from Østerlars to Point C which produces the pentagram. This precise length, when divided by the Golden Section, defines the radius of a circle which will produce a pentagram oriented upon the main Østerlars / Nylars axis and in which Nylars sits in the intersection of the arms of the star.

Figure 14

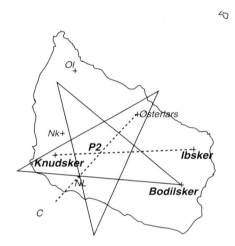

The centre of the pentagram is here labelled P2. The ingenious subtlety employed in determining this position is detailed in Chapter 11. For the purpose of this simplified demonstration, it is sufficient to draw attention to the additional fixing of the design by the placing of the churches of Knudsker and Ibsker to confirm the centre, and the careful positioning of Bodilsker church, which lies exactly upon one apex of the star.

No less than seven churches are required for the fixing of this subtly hidden pentagram. The four round churches have provided the key which gives the shape its size, centre and orientation. Two further churches align meticulously to intersect the centre. The seventh church sits precisely upon one 'horn' of the pentagram.

The precision of the geometry in the production of this Golden Section figure has also provided the Bornholmers with the answer to a long-standing puzzle. In common with all the other mediaeval churches on the island, Bodilsker has an adjacent square stone tower. Its overt purpose was possibly as a watch-tower.

The blatantly phallic symbolism of the 'Devil's Hat', on the tower of Bodilsker church, which is dedicated to the rather obscure English St Botolph.

Built into one of the corners of this tower is a very strange stone, which the islanders have long known as 'The Devil's Hat' and which projects its rounded end from the wall like a phallic fertility symbol. Its presence on the church tower has always been an enigma. Now an explanation is provided. The geometric star-shapes fixed by the placing of Bornholm's churches have all, so far, been tied to the sacred altar. But Bodilsker's pentagram has a different message to impart. The five-pointed star is linked in esoteric symbolism with fertility and magic. And at Bodilsker, it is placed *outside* the church. Bornholm's pentagram is placed *exactly* upon the phallic 'Devil's Hat'.

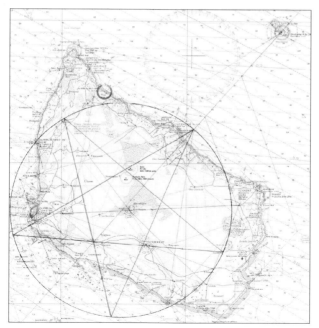

Bornholm and Christiansø with the pentagram overlaid on the map.

Chapter Six
UNITS OF MEASURE

This investigation has, so far, established an interlocking series of geometric figures on the island of Bornholm, whose accuracy can be confirmed by the co-ordinates provided by the Danish Institute for map production, (see Chapter 11). The confirming measurements have, of course, been defined in metres. But the metre unit was unknown to whoever created the original layout. Before continuing with the exploration of the pattern of churches, the question of the unit of measure must be addressed as this will prove to shed yet more, and unexpected, light upon the mystery.

When, in the early 1970s, we stumbled upon the Pentacle of Mountains in the landscape of Rennes-le-Château,[32] the question of a unit of measure being present in the layout did not, at first, arise. However, when David Wood began to extend the original discovery,[33] he noticed that the English mile seemed to fit his findings. As we took the first hesitant steps along this strange pathway, the extreme precision of measure which we were subsequently to encounter, was far from being part of our expectations. Nevertheless, it was immediately evident that Wood's discovery related equally well to the original five mountain peaks.

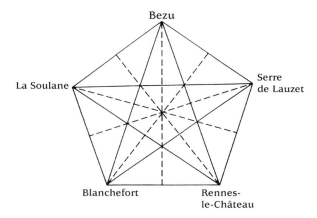

[32] See *The Holy Place* and *Key to the Sacred Pattern.*
[33] See David Wood, *Genisis*, Baton Press, 1985.

It was possible to see that the distances from point to point in the star shape were producing close approximations to round numbers in English miles. Rennes-le-Château to Bezu was four miles, as was Bezu to Blanchefort. Rennes-le-Château and Blanchefort were separated by two and a half miles. This raised a number of matters of interest. The shape was pentagonal and therefore the distances should be in Golden Section relationship to each other. The face of the pentagon (Rennes-le-Château – Blanchefort) should measure the length of the chord (Blanchefort – Bezu) divided by 1.618.

But four miles divided by 1.618 would give 2.472 and not 2.5. On the other hand, if the face was the controlling measure, then 2.5 x 1.618 = 4.045. Only one of the measures could be exact.

But, of course, these mountain peaks are natural landscape features. They were not placed in meaningful relationships by human builders. Nor, as we have said, were we aware of the absolute precision which was later to present itself. There was no necessity to disallow a minor inaccuracy. Nevertheless, the mountains presented so nearly accurate a measure that this was an aspect of the matter which clearly would demand further investigation. But, even without this additional oddity, the structuring of the landscape was itself so unprecedented that it was inevitable, in the early stages of the research, that we should cast about in the most unlikely-seeming of places in the search for enlightenment. Thus we considered the possibility that a clue might be buried in a book published by Bérenger Saunière's friend, the Abbé Boudet, priest of the sister parish of Rennes-les-Bains.

This curious publication, dated 1886, is entitled *La Vraie Langue Celtique* (The True Celtic Tongue). But it also bears the provocative sub-title : *et le Cromleck de Rennes-les-Bains* (and the Cromlech of Rennes-les-Bains). As a cromlech is a landscape feature which appears to have no connection with 'tongues' either Celtic or other, it seemed worth the effort of skimming the work to see if any hint might be forthcoming.

Boudet's book proposed the bizarre thesis that all the languages of humankind are descended from English which was, the author deduced, the tongue spoken by Adam and Eve in the Garden of Eden. The idea is so ludicrous that it appears hardly to merit attention. But Boudet, who died in 1915, is remembered as an erudite priest, whose other writings do not exhibit anything like this degree of eccentricity. Either *La Vraie Langue Celtique* is a mass of nonsensical and irrelevant confusions, or it contains specific information, veiled in a deliberate and subtle way. The latter is a belief firmly held by numerous more-or-less serious treasure-hunters, for whom Boudet's book has become a standard work, reproduced since the late 1970s in several facsimile editions.[34]

---

[34] E.g: Henri Boudet, *La Vraie Langue Celtique*, Belisane, Nice, 1984.

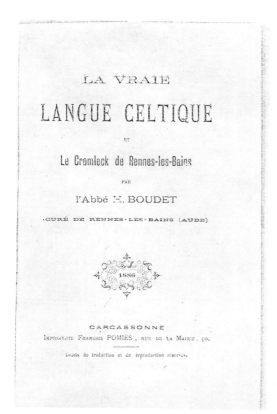

La Vraie Langue Celtique, *the bizarre publication of the Abbé Boudet, friend of Bérenger Saunière.*

Boudet appears to have known something, and given the oddity of the book's subtitle a connection with the new discovery appeared, at the least, possible. The idea, however, that there had been only one primitive universal language and that that language was English, seemed utterly absurd. Nevertheless, in pondering upon what might have led a supposedly intelligent man to make so patently foolish a suggestion, we were led to an interesting thought. No matter what language may be spoken, or written, one is one and two remains two. Whether the manner of inscription be in cuneiform, hieroglyphic, Arabic numerals, or notches upon a stick, the number conveyed by three upraised fingers is recognisable and needs no translation. There is, and always has been, one universal language - and that is Number.

From this simple, but vital, observation grew the suspicion that Boudet's reference to a universal language was not a matter of linguistics, but of numbers. Of course numbers are universal, but a universal language of numbers - numbers within a universal reference scheme - that could only be measure. We hypothesised that Boudet's real hidden message is that, within the English measure system of today, is to be found an universal measure, once understood and used by the earliest civilisations.

Such an idea is certainly odd enough to be rejected by some people without further thought. But in so strange a matter as the Mystery of Rennes-le-Château, any idea, no matter how bizarre, merits at least sufficient consideration to ensure that its rejection is warranted. And the confirmation that the English measure system contains an universal reference is, indeed, to be found in France and specifically in the area of Boudet's activities - the vicinity of Rennes-le-Château. As we have demonstrated, the geometric layout of the churches in the area is based upon an exact measure . . . and that measure is equal to the present English Mile.[35]

If we are right in our interpretation of Boudet's book, then the priest must, obviously, have been aware of the secret of the geometrical layout, as must have been Bertrand de Blanchefort. And via this latter character it could have been employed at Bornholm after his election as Grand Master of the Templars in 1153. Is the English measure discoverable as a reference in the Bornholm layout?

THE METRE, THE YARD AND THE POLE

At the time of the building of the Bornholm churches, we are told, the English yard was fixed as the distance between Henry I's nose and the end of his extended thumb. But, could it be that this popular conception was concealing another truth which was known only to an initiated few - namely that the English measure system, throughout history, has always conformed to an universal reference? This suggestion now seems to the present writers to be not in the least unlikely - it is merely surprising. One very important detail, however, remains to be clarified. If the measure is based upon an universal reference, then what is it? It must surely be something more significant than the bodily proportions of a king.

In *The Holy Place*, we suggested that it is based upon a measurement of the earth's polar circumference; as is our present metric system, which was established in France at the end of the eighteenth century. (The metre is defined as one ten-millionth of a quadrant of the circle which passes through the poles - i.e. one ten-millionth of the distance between the north pole and the equator.) Our later work has substantiated this suggestion. What we termed the 'cromlech' universal reference, is still to be found within the English measure system, and is indeed based upon such a measurement. This can be proved beyond any shadow of doubt. As we shall shortly demonstrate, it is a remarkable fact that, had this been general

[35] See *The Holy Place*, chapter 8.

knowledge, known and understood by the French scientists of the eighteenth century, then the present metre would have been given a slightly greater length. It would then have been a more accurate representation of one ten-millionth of the earth's quadrant.

When, some two hundred years ago, the arc was measured from Dunkirk in France to Barcelona in Spain, a small error was made in the calculations. If, however, the English system had been used, then the error would have been considerably less. The proof of this contention, however, requires an examination of the subdivisions of the English measure system.

THE ENGLISH MEASURE

The mile is divided into various units: the inch; the foot; the yard and the (now little-used) pole, also known as a rod or perch. The relationship between these units is specific:

198 inches	make 1 pole;
320 poles	make 1 mile;
1760 yards	make 1 mile;
5280 feet	make 1 mile;
63360 inches	make 1 mile.

Additionally, 2640 yards make 1 Domesday League - a now forgotten unit of measure which is equal to one and a half miles.

Superficially these numbers appear to be accidental, in the same way that the positioning of the Bornholm churches seems, at first glance, to be accidental. In reality, they are nothing of the kind. We shall show that the English measure system uses these numbers for simple and practical reasons.

Work involving measurement and number is always easier if everything can be expressed in whole numbers. Instructions, especially to an illiterate and innumerate workforce, are much more difficult to explain if one is compelled to deal in fractions which, to those without a knowledge of mathematics, are incomprehensible. There is, however, a practical solution to this problem - and it is demonstrated by the English measure system.

One mile divides into 63360 inches - which seems not to be a very helpful number. But, of course, if you wish to divide it into two equal parts, then each is composed of 31680 inches - still a whole number with no fractions. Divide by two yet again, and still the number is whole - 15840. This operation can be repeated no less than seven times, always resulting in a whole number, the last being 495. And the ingenuity continues. 495 divides into three equal whole-number parts: 165; which again divides into three: 55. And still the whole number divisions continue and provide five equal divisions of 11 inches.

It is true, of course, that the metric system is also divisible by two and by five. Halves, quarters, fifths and tenths are therefore easily produced. But a major disadvantage is that thirds cannot be expressed as whole numbers. One third of a metre can, of course, be given as 33.333 centimetres, or 333.333 millimetres. Such measures can be established, with a satisfactory degree of accuracy when using modern measuring equipment, but it was not always so. Decimal fractions did not begin to filter into common usage until the late sixteenth century, when two pamphlets on the subject, *La Thiende* and *La Disme* were published in 1585, in Holland, by Simon Stevin.

A small but important digression must here be made. The establishment of the 'Statute Mile' is, in itself, an intriguing mystery. It was slipped into English law some few years after Stevin brought the decimal fraction to public notice. Parliament was not sitting in 1592/3 when the definition of the mile was appended - as a complete *non sequitur* - to *'An Acte against newe Buyldinges'*.[36] There seems to be no explanation of why, or by whom, this paragraph was interpolated into an Act of Parliament which makes no other reference to the matter of units of measure.

However, the ingenious and sophisticated flexibility, which is inherent in the number divisions of the mile measure, long predates the sixteenth century. The Rennes-le-Château geometry has clearly hinted at this and the Bornholm layout, fixed as it is upon the island's twelfth century churches, clearly demonstrates the employment of an extremely accurate mile and its subdivisions.

63360 inches to the mile proves to be admirably practical, as the number can be divided into parts of two, three, five and eleven - always providing whole number measures. An extremely convenient and functional system for a designer/architect who needs to give simple instructions to his teams of workers. Stated mathematically, the number 63360 is composed solely of the factors 2, 3, 5 and 11. And these factors are the basis of the other units in the English measure system, as can be seen in the following table:

	2	3	5	11	
Inches in a Pole	2 x	3 x 3 x		11	Equals 198
Poles in a Mile	2 x 2 x 2 x 2 x 2 x 2 x		5		Equals 320
Yards in a Mile	2 x 2 x 2 x 2 x 2 x		5 x	11	Equals 1760
Yards in Domesday League	2 x 2 x 2 x 2 x	3 x	5 x	11	Equals 2640
Feet in a Mile	2 x 2 x 2 x 2 x 2 x	3 x	5 x	11	Equals 5280
Inches in a Mile	2 x 2 x 2 x 2 x 2 x 2 x 2 x	3 x 3 x	5 x	11	Equals 63360

[36] See *Key to the Sacred Pattern* – p 209.

One is led to the conclusion that the numbers were carefully selected for practical reasons. Unquestionably, they provide a simple means of dividing the unit of measure into 2, 3 and 5 parts; which are divisions used frequently in building and architecture. Another interesting question is also raised. The factor 11 is clearly a part of each subdivision (with the exception of the number of Poles in a Mile). It is this property, unique to the English system, which gives the numbers their odd appearance. Why was it important to divide the unit measure into eleven parts?

It seemed worth considering the possibility that this oddity might shed some light upon the suggestion that Boudet's *Vraie Langue Celtique* could be referring to an original universal language of measure, seemingly exclusive to the English measure system. We were thus obliged to take two steps. Firstly, to examine why the English system is constructed as it is. Secondly, to attempt to discover if any measure systems from remote antiquity might show this same peculiarity. If this should prove to be the case, then we could well be upon the track of an early universal system.

Let us summarise what we have thus far found: the English measure system is so constructed that it is simply subdivided into elements which are frequently used - for example in architecture. The instructions for the raising of a building may easily be expressed in simple whole numbers, i.e. halves, thirds and fifths. But this system also employs the factor eleven. Why eleven? Could there be any practical reason for an easy division into eleven parts?

Such a division proves, in fact, to be of a very important and practical use. Within the system, it is possible to measure the circumference of a circle and still use whole numbers. To do so, it is necessary to realise that twenty-two sevenths is a very good approximation of pi - and twenty-two is equal to two times eleven. The English measure system seems to indicate that this fact was known to its inventors. The system can only properly be understood in relation to this explanation, which proves thus to be logical in all details. In practice it works as follows: Should you wish to construct a circle with a circumference of one mile, then the radius will be 280 yards - or 840 feet - or 10080 inches. All whole numbers. And it works equally well with all the basic fractions.

If the intended circumference is one third of a mile (1760 feet) - the radius is 280 feet.

With a circumference of one fifth of a mile - 352 yards - the radius is 56 yards.

A circumference of one thirtieth of a mile - 176 feet - has a radius of 28 feet.

One thirty sixth of a mile - 1760 inches - can be constructed with a radius of 280 inches.

And thus, the three hundred and sixtieth part of a mile (one degree of the original circle - 176 inches - can be constructed using a radius of 28 inches.

All these measures - circumference, fractions of the circumference and radius - can be expressed in whole numbers.

This is extraordinary. Without the factors two, three, five and eleven, the calculations would have been very complicated and the numbers extremely uneasy. But, can we find any evidence of these neat and tidy English round mile measures in the Bornholm System?

On page 50 above, we have pointed out that the official co-ordinates give the Østerlars / Nylars measure - the controlling radius - as about 14336 metres. The original radius must have been somewhere very close to this distance. In English measure, this is very close indeed to 15680 yards, or eight miles and sixteen hundred yards. Sixteen hundred yards is an interesting fraction of a mile ... it is ten elevenths. The tell-tale eleven has appeared.

If this is indeed the carefully chosen radius of a circle, then what is its circumference? As our schoolday memories may remind us, the circumference of a circle is measured as the radius times two times pi - ($2\pi r$). Using the 'simple pi' of twenty-two sevenths the formula is:

$$15680 \text{ yards} \times 2 = 31360$$
$$31360 \times 22 = 689920$$
$$689920 \div 7 = 98560 \text{ yards}$$

All whole numbers - even the division by seven. **And 98560 yards make exactly fifty-six miles.**

(An interesting additional aspect of this carefully chosen distance is the fact that, even when expressed in metres the 'whole number' element remains:

$$14336 \times 2 = 28672$$
$$28672 \times 22 = 630784$$
$$630784 \div 7 = 90112$$

It seems that we may have found the explanation for the use of the factor eleven in the English measure system and thus have established that the 'fathers' of the system must have known, and used, the fraction twenty-two sevenths as a practical solution to pi. ($14336 = 7 \times 2^{11}$).

This brilliantly chosen circle radius generates yet more figures whose dimensions can be measured in 'round English miles'. On page 60 above, we have described how it leads to the square-root seven triangle – the symbol of Spiritual Wisdom. The area of this triangle – with an accuracy better than one part in a thousand – is equal to the area of a rectangle which has one side equal to the prime circle radius (15680 yards) and the other side measuring the round figure of exactly twenty-seven miles.

The circumference of the square-root seven triangle – with an accuracy better than one part in ten thousand – is equal to the circumference of a square with a diagonal of exactly twenty-five miles.

If this square is doubled to form a rectangle, then its area will be exactly six hundred and twenty-five square miles – and this is equal to the area of a square with sides of twenty-five miles.

(Readers interested in the exact calculations will find them in the following box.)

The formula to calculate the area of the square-root seven triangle is:
(horizontal) $\sqrt{7} : 2$ multiplied by (vertical) $(\sqrt{7} : \sqrt{3}) \times (3 : 2)$
Thus the **area** of this particular triangle will be:
((8 miles 1600 yards) = **15680** yards multiplied by $(\sqrt{7} : 2)$ multiplied by 15680 yards multiplied by $(\sqrt{7} : \sqrt{3}) \times (3 : 2) = 20742.69028$ yards x 35927.39345 yards = 745230794.8 square yards

This is equal to the area of a rectangle having one side of 27 miles (47520 yards) whose other side will be (745230794.8 : 47520)
= **15682.46622** yards.

Difference from circle radius: (15682.466 – 15680 =) 2.47 yards.
Percentage deviation: 0.015.

The **circumference** of the square-root triangle is:
(8 miles 1600 yards =) 15680 yards multiplied $\sqrt{7}$ multiplied by 3 =
124456.1417 yards.

The circumference of a square with diagonal of 25 miles is (4 x 25 = 100 miles =) 176000 yards divided by $\sqrt{2}$ = **124450.7935** yards.

Difference: 5.35 yards. **Percentage deviation: 0.004.**

The side of the above square is its diagonal divided by $\sqrt{2}$ (25 : $\sqrt{2}$).
The rectangle, being the double square will have one side equal to the square and the other side of double length.

Multiplying the two sides of this rectangle to find its area, we have:
(25 : $\sqrt{2}$ x 50 : $\sqrt{2}$ = (25 x 50) : ($\sqrt{2}$ x $\sqrt{2}$) = 25 x 50 : 2 = 625 **square miles.**
This is equal to a square with the side being the square-root of 625 = **25 miles.**

GRAIL SIDELIGHT

The triangle, symbolic of spiritual wisdom, has shown how it can conjoin with other geometric figures - specifically, the circle, the square and the rectangle. These three simple basic shapes lead, unexpectedly, to a faint and evocative echo of the Holy Grail. How?

In pursuing the hunt for an understanding of this shadowy story, it was inevitable that we should encounter the connections between the Templars and that mysterious object, the Holy Grail. Inevitable, too, that we should devote some time to the search for any possible light which might be shed upon this other, and equally mysterious, object. Even though it seemed, at first, to be a separate, and peripheral, issue, the Bornholm Grail quest was to provide provocative questions.

It is interesting, in the context of the present research, to note that the first reference to the Grail dates from about 1185; the time when the Templars were at the height of their power; the time of the building of the great Gothic cathedrals; the time of the planning of the Baltic Mission. The time when the Order - if, indeed, it possessed a body of precious and secret knowledge - would have been best able to put it into practise.

The first Grail story - *Le Conte du Graal* - (there were many more to follow), was written by Chrétien de Troyes. As his name implies, he came from the town of Troyes, and he was connected to the court of the Count of Champagne. He was therefore moving in those same circles where the Knights Templar originated and which were so closely linked to St Bernard de Clairvaux and the Burgundian nobility.

But what is the Grail? For most people the word conjures the image of a gleaming, sacred chalice. The mystical 'something' sought by the Knights of the Round Table. Perhaps the cup used by Jesus at the Last Supper - or in which his blood was caught as he hung upon the Cross. For some it is that fabled object, the Philosopher's Stone, so coveted by the mediaeval alchemists. Or perhaps the Blood of Jesus in an allegorical sense, the Sang Raal, his blood descent?[37] These are among the best known of the present interpretations. The Grail, however, may be just one of them. Or all of them. Or perhaps it is something quite different. Certainly, many curious suggestions have been made by many different students of the Grail stories.

In his book on Chartres Cathedral, Louis Charpentier cites a most strange and cryptic quotation, which he describes as 'a traditional riddle':

> *Trois tables ont porté le Graal : une table ronde, une table carrée et une table rectangulaire. Toutes les trois ont la meme surface et leur Nombre est 21. ...*
> Three tables bore the Grail - one table round, one table square, and one table rectangular. All three have the same surface and their Number is 21.

Could there be an answer to this strange riddle? Again we find ourselves dealing with shape - and number. What numerical and/or geometrical aspect can there possibly be to the Holy Grail? We are confronting a complicated metaphor which may have many interpretations, some more likely than others. But one of them appears to be undeniably geometric: 'Three Tables bore the Grail' ... What can this mean?

In the island's geometry, we have identified a controlling circle with an enclosed square and a small appended triangle (Figure 6, page 52). We have also found a larger circle (Figure 12, page 60) enclosing a triangle whose sides relate to the square root of seven. A triangle, of course, has three sides. Three times seven is 21.

---

[37] For a development of this hypothesis, see *The Holy Blood and the Holy Grail.*

Could the cryptic reference to 21 be a hint? Could it symbolise a triangle whose sides are not 'seven' , but the mystic 'square root of seven'?

This is not merely a long shot . . . it is also, undeniably, a shot in the dark, and a wild one, at that. Firstly - the riddle refers to geometric figures: square, circle and rectangle - but not to a triangle. Secondly, there is no mention of square-root seven - nor even of seven. The reference is clearly to 21. And lastly, the circumference of a square-root seven triangle - three times square root seven $(3 \times \sqrt{7})$ - is not even the square root of 21, but is the square root of 63!

'Their Number is 21', says the riddle. This enigma remains. 21, however, can be looked upon as a simple reference to the significance of numbers. It is the sum of the first six 'rational' numbers: $1 + 2 + 3 + 4 + 5 + 6 = 21$.

Square-root seven, however, symbolises spiritual wisdom. The Templars, we are told, worshipped an idol called Baphomet and this, as Hugh Schonfield brilliantly proved, is the enciphered name *Sophia* - 'Wisdom'.[38]

On Bornholm we have found links between the Templars and the mediaeval churches. We have found the evidence of unexpected skills in mathematics, geometry and geodesy in the precision of the layout of those churches in the landscape. It is impossible to avoid the conclusion that the Templars were aware of the significance of the pattern underlying their endeavours. In some sense, the Templars were shaping the landscape to conform to a body of knowledge which they kept jealously to themselves. But why should they wish to lay out star-patterns across the island? The patterns, after all, are invisible.

The questions and the hypotheses proliferate. Were they mirroring the layout of constellations? Were they leading us to the hiding place of a treasure? Were they preparing locations for heretical rituals? New-age mystics might suggest that they were, perhaps, harnessing the earth's energy. Or ... ? The wishful-thinking is too easily encouraged by such mysteries.

But the incredible work was not only skilled. It was laborious; it was time-consuming; it was serious. It was not a game. These fierce warrior monks would not have wasted their energies on whimsical exercises. Whatever they were doing had a sober and practical purpose, but the entire history of the Order trails with it the scent of secrecy. Whether in their mysterious delving beneath the soil of Jerusalem, or in their building of mathematically controlled churches, they were clearly pursuing a goal that seems to us, so far, incomprehensible. They had knowledge. They 'worshipped' *Sophia*. And Wisdom must be preserved if it cannot be imparted.

The riddle of the Grail may still rest, for the time, unsolved. But Bornholm has shown that an impressive knowledge of number and measure was being recorded

[38] See: Hugh Schonfield, *The Essene Odyssey*, Element Books, 1984.

- albeit invisibly. The English measure and a knowledge of pi have already revealed themselves. But this cannot be all that the 'fathers' of this system have to teach us. And it is their use of the English measure which leads to the next step. It demonstrates that they based their system upon an exact measurement of the circumference of the earth.

EARTH MEASURE

In our book *The Holy Place,* we suggested that the English pole measure (also known as the rod or perch) was in some way related to the measurement of the earth. This has proved to be a more reliable guess than was realised at the time.

The term 'pole' is itself suggestive. Could it imply that this particular unit of measure is, in some way, related to the polar circumference of the earth - as is our present metre? The answer to this question is: yes. Though this only became clear as a result of the above analysis. The English measure system can be shown to demonstrate an extremely ingenious relationship between the pole unit and the earth's circumference.

A circle with the circumference of one pole (198 inches), as demonstrated in the above system - has a diameter of 63 inches. Once again, of course, a whole number - but this time, a most essential number. This diameter proves to be equal to one twenty-five millionth of the earth's polar circumference, and so exactly that there can be little doubt that the pole measure must be defined from this measurement. This, it seems, is the basic relationship which defines all the units of the English measure system.[39]

The metre was defined, at the end of eighteenth century, as one forty millionth of the earth's polar circumference. It follows, therefore, that the circumference should be forty million metres. Unfortunately, when the measurement was originally calculated, a small error was made. NASA presently gives the circumference as 40,007,476 metres - 7,476 metres longer than the definition made by French scientists two centuries ago. Had those eighteenth century scientists simply multiplied the English 63 inch 'pole circle diameter' by 25 million, they would have arrived at a considerably better result :

$$63 \times 25000000 = 1575000000 \text{ (inches)} \div 63360 = 24857.954 \text{ (miles)}$$
$$= 40,003,905 \text{ metres.}$$

The two hundred year old error is almost halved.

---

[39] The units of the English measure have varied at different times and in different places. Our references to the 'foot', 'pole', 'mile' etc are, for the purposes of this enquiry, to be understood as the presently given definitions, enshrined in the 1592/3 Statute (see page 138). This curious Act of Parliament seems to have perpetuated an ancient system which has remained consistent since remote times.

There remains yet another interesting aspect of the English measure. The creators of the metre decided to base it upon the distance from the pole to the equator - one fourth of the earth's circumference. The creators of the English system, however, chose to base their unit upon a one fifth division of the earth's circumference. Thus, were it not for the eighteenth century error, five 'pole-diameters' of 63 inches should equate with 8 metres. Five times 63 inches is, however, equal to 8.001 metres - 1 millimetre longer than the present distance defined as 8 metres.

This means that, while the metre is based upon a quadragesimal division of the surface of the earth, the English measure is based upon a pentagonal division of the same surface.

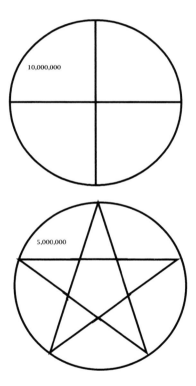

This is fascinatingly in accordance with the ancient symbolic value attributed to the numbers. A division of four relates to Matter - i.e. Earth. On the other hand, a pentagonal division relates to Man. The English measure system is thus based not merely upon the dimensions of the earth, but is also symbolic of Man's relationship with it.

SYMBOLIC PRECISION

Although the system can be explained as both rational and practical, it seems rather a complicated procedure to use the circumference of the (pole-)circle as the main measure. There must be a reason for this choice. The unique English subdivisions compensate admirably for the difficulties occasioned by such a definition - and indeed has turned them to advantage. But the effort involved seems unwonted. Unless there is another, and important, consideration. And the English measure system proves to express yet another philosophical concept, based upon an exact knowledge of nature and manifested in its definition.

It is important first to realise that there is something about the earth, which the fathers of the measure system seemed to consider as the embodiment of a philosophical and religious idea. In philosophical terms, life and death are expressions of change. Mortal life is 'a step'. Life and death equate with the changes of night into day, or summer into winter. But there is also a factor of stability in nature: there is eternity – there is God.

Our planet can be regarded as an embodiment of both these concepts. The equator moves constantly, causing day to change into night and back again into day. The axis of the earth through the poles, on the other hand, appears never to change. Stability is expressed in the way that the measure system relates to the polar circumference in the length of unit significantly termed a pole.

But all is so brilliantly contrived that there is also an ingenious connection with the exact measurement of the moving factor which is the earth's equatorial circumference. The relationship between the English pole and the English foot is subtly chosen to express the pole's link with the polar circumference, while the foot is expressing its association with the equatorial circumference.

The equatorial circumference of the earth is greater than is the polar circumference from which the metre is derived. The difference is substantial. It is 66,680 metres (41 miles, 762 yards = 218,766 feet). The manner in which the foot measure relates to and expresses the greater equatorial circumference is closely linked to the philosophical concepts of life and change.

In order to demonstrate this fact, the equatorial circumference must first be divided into 360 degrees. Each degree is then divided into as many parts as there are days in 1000 years. Each of those days is then represented by the length of one foot. Thus ingeniously does the foot division of space relate to the millennial division of time. The symbolism is both simple and significant. And the accuracy is beyond coincidence.

Not only does this calculation require a knowledge of the equatorial circumference of the earth, it is also necessary to have a knowledge of the number of days in a year. If the length of a year is defined as 365.2 days, then the calculation gives:

1000 (years) multiplied by 360 (degrees) multiplied by 365.2 (days) = 131472000.

NASA gives the equatorial measure as 40074156 metres, which is equal to 131476890 feet.

The discrepancy is no more than 4890 feet, or 1630 yards - less than one mile from absolute perfection.

The English measure system thus provides evidence that, in the remote past, the earth was measured with astonishing accuracy. Where, when and by whom, was this mastery of number and measure developed? Why have we remained unaware of these skills, which must have been acquired by laborious and painstaking observations over many, many years? And why, even today, are some scholars still reluctant to face these facts? For facts they are. Why do they cause unease? Is it truly so difficult to accept that we are not that far advanced beyond our 'ignorant' predecessors?

No less important than the knowledge itself is the fact that, down the centuries, certain people, it seems, have retained it as privileged information. Many of the ideas which form part of this lost wisdom would once, of course, have been held by the Church to be heresy. As Galileo found, such information can be dangerous. One can understand the reluctance to promulgate these ideas at certain periods in the history of our civilisation. But why now? For a century or more such enlightenment would have been welcomed, or at least examined and debated. Nevertheless, it seems that this lore has never been lost - if the oblique hints in Boudet's book, which led to this research, are to be considered valid. The hints may be doubtful, but the conclusions are not.

Part Two

BELIEFS

**L'hypothèse est
la poésie des sciences**

(Hypothesis is the poetry of science)
Henri Poincaré

Chapter Seven
UNRAVELLING
A COMPLEX PATTERN

We have been following an apparently meandering course, wandering from Scandinavian history, through religious faith and secret societies to mathematics and complex geometry. It is time to attempt to draw, as it were, a map of the separate byways which we have traversed, in order to understand the unknown country into which we have strayed. We must attempt to verify that these different paths have all spread out from one central 'citadel'. We must create an hypothesis which will make sense of the confusions.

Of one thing we can be sure. Our citadel rests on firm foundations. The precision of the Bornholm mathematics and geometry cannot be gainsaid. Certainly, there will be those who will insist on crying 'Coincidence' - but such objections are merely wishful-thinking based upon ignorance of the facts and can be ignored. The rock upon which we stand is the unquestionable demonstration of the employment of highly sophisticated skills in a distant past. A body of knowledge which has been lost and is now re-found - at least in part. A body of knowledge whose previous possessors have remained always in the shadows, but of whom we have gained the occasional and tantalising glimpse. The Knights Templar, or at least some of them, must have known it. The Templars seem to have been involved in the building of the Bornholm churches, and certainly, whoever chose the sites for those churches must have known it. How deep was the involvement of Bernard of Clairvaux? Of Bertrand de Blanchefort? Of Archbishop Eskil?

But, of course, the geometry of Bornholm is no more than part of the secret wisdom which we are uncovering. The pyramid builders shared it - as did the devisers of the English measure system. Even the Abbé Boudet seems to have known it. But now the certainty begins to change to mere suspicion. Did Saunière know? It is likely - but no more. Did Helena, mother of the Emperor Constantine know? Did King Charles XIII find and pass on to the Swedish Freemasons, a genuine secret knowledge which still they will not share? Now, again, we can sense quicksands beneath our feet.

Our citadel of certainty lies in a *terra incognita,* surrounded by a strange landscape which is enveloped in mist and confusing shadows. It would appear that the knowledge which we have been uncovering must have been known - if not always fully understood - and transmitted continuously, in one form or another, through many long centuries. Shrouded in myth and legend, belief and faith, it has surfaced at various times and in various places. It has been hinted at and obfuscated, accepted and rejected, mocked and lied about, upheld on faith alone and dismissed on equally tenuous grounds.

But it cannot now be denied that the knowledge is there, waiting to be drawn into the light. We have found a clearly defined pathway of number and pattern which can, in no sense, be described as imaginary. It is too precise, too clear, too clever, too complex to be a mere fantasy. What possibilities, then, lie in the hints and myths, legends and beliefs which lie along our trail? Where to begin the search?

It is impossible to be certain at what date, or from whence, came the origins of the lost knowledge we are seeking. The fact that standing stones, which date from Megalithic times, seem to be associated with the geometric configurations to be found on Bornholm, as well as at Rennes-le-Château, implies that those origins may lie further back in time than seems, at first, to be likely. The churches which gave the first hints of the work may, perhaps, have been usurping earlier sacred sites. But, at least, we can be certain that the geometry has been laid out on Bornholm since the twelfth century at latest and at Rennes-le-Château from a century or so earlier. The church structures which define the patterns bear solid witness to this fact. Christianity has certainly played its part in preserving the knowledge in its enduring legacy of buildings. It is here, therefore, with the first signs of the church upon our trail, that we will begin.

THE HOLY SEPULCHRE

In Chapter Three we have referred to the curious matter of the identification, in the fourth century, of the burial place of Jesus by Helena, mother of the Emperor Constantine. The Church of the Holy Sepulchre is now unquestionably accepted as marking the true location. Some historians may, perhaps, raise small doubts, but in general, for the multitudes of the faithful, belief has served as proof. The question is no longer raised.

We must consider what people have believed, or have said that they believed, concerning Helena's chosen site and the reasons for her choice. We are told that she was blessed with a dream, or vision, which led her to the Holy Sepulchre. In this modern, sceptical age, no great reliability is accorded to such techniques of detection. The explanation seems inherently unlikely.

However, verisimilitude plays no part in this examination - we are dealing with belief alone. After all, it is also inherently unlikely that a man should be born of a virgin, or walk upon water. But in any consideration of the Christian faith we must

Late nineteenth century view of the church of the
Holy Sepulchre, Jerusalem.

accept such propositions as forming part of the basis of our enquiry. Even beliefs about beliefs have a part to play. For example, the emphasis which the Catholic church places upon the idea of the 'virginity' of Mary, the mother of Jesus. Virginity is not extraordinary *per se*, after all, the state is a common one. All women are born virgin.

The perpetual virginity of Mary has, not surprisingly, created problems for many believers. This has led to a desire for an 'explanation'. And, in one sense, Mary can be said to have remained a Virgin, despite her motherhood. It has been suggested that a tradition of dynastic marriage would have ensured that her birth occurred under the astrological sign of Virgo. Dynastic marriages, it is claimed, were so arranged and controlled that offspring might be born under Virgo. The marriage of Joachim and Anna, the parents of Mary, supposedly also conforms to this pattern. Such ideas drift across the seas of belief and, lacking proof, must be considered just as valid as any other. The faithful have always readily accepted that Mary was Virgin and that same acceptance must be brought to the no less uncertain beliefs of those who have laid the foundations of our puzzle. With this borne in mind, then, what questions have been raised - and what beliefs have been expressed - concerning the death, burial and sepulchre of Jesus and the dream or vision which led to its rediscovery by Helena?

Matthew (27, 57) tells us that:
When the even was come, there came a rich man of Arimathea, named Joseph, who also himself was Jesus' disciple: He went to Pilate, and begged the body of Jesus. Then Pilate commanded the body to be delivered. And when Joseph had taken the body, he wrapped it in a clean linen cloth, and laid it in his own new tomb, which he had hewn out in the rock ...

John (19, 38-42) expands the story:
.... Joseph of Arimathea, being a disciple of Jesus, but secretly for fear of the Jews, besought Pilate that he might take away the body of Jesus: And Pilate gave him leave. He came therefore, and took the body of Jesus. And there came also Nicodemus, which at the first came to Jesus by night, and brought a mixture of myrrh and aloes, about an hundred pound weight. Then took they the body of Jesus, and wound it in linen clothes with the spices, as the manner of the Jews is to bury. Now in the place where he was crucified there was a garden; and in the garden a new sepulchre, wherein was never man yet laid. There laid they Jesus therefore because of the Jews preparation day; for the sepulchre was nigh at hand.

One must first ask, why was Joseph of Arimathea so eager to take charge of the body of Jesus and why should he wish to place it in this particular cave? From the above accounts, it is clear that two people, Joseph and Nicodemus, are responsible for the preparation of the body and for its burial. Neither of them has previously been mentioned in the Gospels as being numbered among the disciples who, one might have thought, as his closest friends, were more likely to have assumed these duties. Unless, perhaps, they were closer than merely friends.

In such matters, of course, it would be yet more usual for the immediate family to make the funeral arrangements and some commentators have suggested that Joseph of Arimathea may have been Joses, the younger brother of Jesus, who is mentioned in Matthew 13, 55. Strangely, it still seems difficult for many people to accept the idea that Jesus had brothers and sisters, as this seems to accord ill with the emphasis which the Catholic Church lays upon the virginity of Mary. But Jesus is more than once referred to as Mary's 'firstborn', which would be an altogether unnecessary distinction if he were her only child. (There are also several direct references to the brothers and sisters of Jesus:- Mark 6, 3. Matthew 13, 55 and John 6, 42.)

Indeed, on reflection, it is interesting to note that the Gospel accounts make no reference to any relatives of Jesus being involved in these most personal and familial of responsibilities, even though they are clear that his mother was present at his crucifixion. This is especially curious given the fact that the Jews have strict rules concerning mourning and the duties of a bereaved family. And, although such niceties may not have been of any concern to Pilate, he certainly appears to accede readily enough to Joseph's request to remove the body. Joseph must, therefore, presumably have had some rights in the matter.

To compound the problem of the identity of Joseph of Arimathea, it has also been proposed that he was not Jesus' younger brother Joses, but was rather another brother - James. This personage, also known as James the Just, was the leader of the first church in Jerusalem, instituted after the crucifixion of Jesus. We are told that James the Just was stoned in AD 62 and was succeeded as leader of the church by Simon, son of Cleophas - apparently a first cousin of Jesus. According to some[40], stoning was not necessarily a capital punishment, but was a symbolic act and part of a ceremony of expulsion. This explanation enables James the Just to reappear in Glastonbury as Joseph of Arimathea, complete with Holy Thorn.

But what of Nicodemus? The Bible mentions him only briefly. We learn that he is a 'ruler of the Jews', a personage of some importance, a member of the Sanhedrin, the Jewish ruling council. He 'comes to Jesus by night'. The implication seems to be that the meeting was clandestine - perhaps Nicodemus' position as 'a ruler of the Jews' prevents him from visiting Jesus openly. He questions Jesus on his miracles, (John 3,2): 'Rabbi, we know that thou art a teacher come from God, for no man can do these miracles that thou doest, except God be with him.'

But, instead of giving a simple confirmatory response that, yes, indeed, his power does come from God, Jesus makes a curious statement: 'Verily, verily, I say unto thee, Except a man be born again, he cannot see the kingdom of God.'

It is possible that this is meant to be interpreted in an allegorical fashion, as an explanation for the miracles - but Nicodemus seems not to understand: 'How can a man be born when he is old? Can he enter the second time into his mother's womb, and be born?'

Jesus replies with a lengthy explanation concerning rebirth, not 'of the flesh', but 'of water and of the spirit'. This can only be understood as an allegorical description of a ritual rebirth - in other words, a sort of initiation. And when Nicodemus still seems not to understand, Jesus taunts him: 'Art thou a master of Israel, and knowest not these things?'

He continues with yet more explanation, this time with the important initiatory understanding of the distinction between metaphorical light and darkness. Whether, this explanation enables Nicodemus finally to understand the meaning of Jesus' words, is not made clear.

Apart from one brief later mention, when Nicodemus speaks in defence of Jesus before the Pharisees, this is all that the Gospels tell us of him. Claims have been made, however, that both Nicodemus and Joseph of Arimathea can be identified as having been present at the strange event known as 'The Transfiguration'.

---

[40] E.g. Laurence Gardner, *Bloodline of the Holy Grail*.

(Mark 9, 2-4):

> And after six days, Jesus taketh with him Peter, and James, and John, and leadeth them up into an high mountain apart by themselves; and he was transfigured before them. And his raiment became shining, exceeding white as snow; so as no fuller on earth can white them. And there appeared unto them Elias with Moses: and they were talking with Jesus.

Is this curious incident to be accepted as a simple factual account? What is its significance? And how does it concern Nicodemus and Joseph of Arimathea? Along the curious byways opened up during these researches, we encountered an eighteenth-century German theologian, named J.A. Starck, who claimed to have had access to 'secret' information, which renders explicable this strange and apparently supernatural Transfiguration of Jesus.

STARCK'S CLERICAL

Starck was highly educated, widely travelled and the respected Chaplain at the Court of Weimar. He was also an acknowledged expert in Oriental linguistics. Suddenly, in 1767, he announced that he was Chaplain to the Knights Templar. An extraordinary claim, as the Order, as far as anybody knew, had supposedly been suppressed in the early years of the fourteenth century.

The Templars had been authorised, by Pope Alexander III in 1172, to appoint their own priests. According to Starck, these priests were an inner and secret group within the Order and were directly descended from the Canons of the Holy Sepulchre in Jerusalem. This secret group called themselves The League of Canonical Knights of the Holy Sepulchre in Jerusalem of Our Lord Jesus Christ's Holy and Poor Templar Order.

Starck seems to have re-established this League openly as a kind of Freemasonic Order, which he called 'Starck's Clerical'. His secret documents were never made available to Freemasonry in general, and their very existence would have remained seriously in question, were it not for the Swedish King Charles XIII, who gained access to them. Charles, it should be remembered, subsequently established the curious Swedish Masonic System and it is in their archive that Starck's documents now reside.

Starck's mysterious secret documents apparently give an explanation of what is claimed to be the true nature of the Transfiguration and of what really took place on the mountain. The three disciples, Peter, James and John, Starck would have us believe, were undergoing a ceremony of initiation. Again according to Starck, the Templars knew of a secret hierarchy within the disciples of Jesus. This hierarchy was divided into groups of three. At the time of the Transfiguration, Jesus had already initiated, through a 'ritual re-birth', both his brother Joses / Joseph and Nicodemus, who had visited him by night with such pertinent questions.

The Starck documents assure us that James, Peter and John did not, of course, see the spirits of Moses and Elijah. It seems that no supernatural beings took part in the Transfiguration. What the disciples really saw was Jesus in the company of Joseph of Arimathea and Nicodemus. The latter two are present because, having already been initiated, they have a role to play in the initiation of the new group. James, Peter and John are ritually 're-born' in some form of arcane rite and thus gain access to certain secrets. These secrets teach liberation from the ties of matter; the practical means to salvation; how man may use his liberated, divine power to master both the natural and the spiritual worlds and to enter into 'a new heaven and a new earth'.[41]

If we are to believe Starck's account, then Joseph and Nicodemus are Jesus' two most trusted disciples - an inner circle in his apparently partly clandestine organisation. And this - with the possible family relationship of at least one of them - explains why these two alone take over the arrangements for his burial.

Yet another element in this story, encountered upon the masonic / Templar pathway, is a custom, apparently current in some secret societies. It would appear that the most precious of a group's possessions were kept concealed in a vault in or near the Grand Master's grave. Such a tradition, it has been suggested, forms part of the puzzle concerning the sepulchre of Jesus.

But how do these curious claims relate to the discovery of the Tomb by Helena, the mother of Constantine? This odd admixture of historical, biblical, and masonic elements can be pulled together to provide a hypothetical explanation for otherwise inexplicable visions, dreams, beliefs and even actions, which have floated to the surface of this muddy pool.

SCENARIO

From the forgoing accounts, then, as well as other fragments which have been encountered throughout this investigation, it is possible to produce the following simple, if fragile, plot-line:

Jesus is part of - or has created - a sect of some sort, which includes elements of initiatory practise and therefore secret, or at least, hidden knowledge.

Joseph of Arimathea, perhaps a close relative, possibly a brother of Jesus, is part of his inner confraternity and is especially concerned with the arrangements for Jesus' burial in his own newly-built tomb.

Helena, mother of Constantine, is a descendant of Joseph of Arimathea and is thus in possession of secrets handed down in her family. These enable her to identify Jesus' tomb, three centuries after his burial.

[41] Sverre Dag Mogstad, *Frimureri*, Universitetsforlaget, Oslo, 1994.

With Jerusalem in Constantine's hands, Helena gains undisturbed access to the burial place and thus to the secrets concealed therein by her ancestor, Joseph of Arimathea. Her son then ensures the future security of the hiding place by constructing upon it the Church of the Holy Sepulchre.

In the twelfth century, the Templars, in their turn, gain undisturbed access to the hiding place. In the Church of the Holy Sepulchre, they take the vows which institute their Order. Their avowed task is the protection of the pilgrims upon the highways to the holy places of Palestine, but there is no evidence to demonstrate in what manner, if at all, the tiny group of nine men were able to carry out this mammoth operation. Evidence does exist, however, that they expended an enormous amount of labour in clearing the so-called Stables of Solomon, beneath the Temple Mount. And after nine years their Grand Master, Hugues de Payens, informs St Bernard that 'their task is accomplished'.

These threads appear to form part of Starck's version of events. His ideas were unquestionably a major influence upon King Charles XIII and his establishment of the Swedish System of Freemasonry.

Again, it must be emphasised that it matters not at all if these ideas are likely, or even credible. It is more important to remember that Charles XIII appears to have paid particular attention to Starck's claim to be a member of the secret Order of Knights Templar. We must therefore accept his belief - or at least his wish to believe - that the Templars must still have been in existence and were still in possession of the secret body of knowledge. Charles' library also held documents purporting to establish the continuation of the Templar Order after the burning of its last Grand Master, Jacques de Molay .

A peculiarity of Charles' masonic system, which is of particular interest, relates to initiation into the eighth degree, when the member is admitted as a Knight Templar. The Scandinavian System insists that this is the real, but covert, continuation of the original, mediaeval Order and demonstrates what purports to be a most important link with the first Templars. The system has a clandestine organisation within the organisation. This hidden group is known only to those who are accorded the privilege of joining the inner circle.

Overtly, the System is composed of twelve degrees. The crucial point is reached at the tenth degree, where a secret selection is made. All brothers who are admitted to the tenth degree believe that they have passed the examination which is part of the admission ritual. But in reality, most have failed the significant but covert test. Only a very few are selected and these then go through another and different form of initiation. Only to these chosen few is given the knowledge of their special status. Thereafter they continue their way through the system by way of entry into a hidden level of the eleventh degree.

These especially chosen brothers are the ones who form the interior fraternity. They are the group referred to by Starck as The League of Canonical Knights of the

Holy Sepulchre in Jerusalem of Our Lord Jesus Christ's Holy and Poor Templar Order. Charles XIII's confidential documents describe these Canonical Knights as a 'secret brotherhood within the brotherhood, forever united with the Templar Order. Those in possession of this knowledge are a closed and secret fraternity, unknown to other brothers.' When in session, the League is referred to as the Sanhedrin and the Master is accorded the title of Father of Wisdom. He refers to the secret brothers as his Beloved Sons.[42]

The Swedish Freemasonic System has, from its inception, enjoyed the protection of the royal houses of Scandinavia and continues to do so to the present day. In Sweden itself, the position of Grand Master has been held by the monarch, from the original foundation by King Gustav III and his brother King Charles XIII, to the death of the late King Gustav VI Adolf. Only the present King Charles XVI Gustav has refused to become a Freemason.

The above résumé is based upon the work of Sverre Dag Mogstad, who has gained access to the archive. It suggests that, at least in the eyes of Swedish Freemasonry, there has been a continuous transmission of secrets, (perhaps viewed as knowledge - certainly held as belief), down the centuries and leading back to the Templars - and possibly beyond. The Templars, then, seem always to lurk in the shadows of this mystery and their equivocal story adds a curious under-layer to other tantalising possibilities. Five hundred years after the apparent end of their Order, there comes another faint echo of their activities.

BENEATH JERUSALEM

We have made mention, in Chapter Three, of Johan Millén, a Swedish engineer who, in the early years of the twentieth century, led an English expedition to Jerusalem. This venture, known as the Parker Expedition, was privately financed by an organisation registered as JMPFW Ltd.

Millén and his team performed a task which seems curiously to echo the Templars' activities. They spent many months burrowing beneath the ground - and Millén himself later admitted that, behind their ostensible purpose lay a secret, hidden agenda. What could this have been? Before this question can be answered, we must consider the climate of general scholarly enquiry in which Millén was working.

Historians had long been bringing a more scientific approach to the study of the foundations of faith. Interest had grown and with it the desire of the educated laity to learn more of the real world in which the events of the Biblical narratives had

[42] Sverre Dag Mogstad op cit.

taken place. Of direct relevance to the apparent purpose of Millén's expedition was the considerable academic debate, which was current at the end of the nineteenth century, concerning the precise identity of Mount Zion. Equally uncertain was which, of the several hills of Jerusalem, was the true 'City of David'? Jerusalem had been so thoroughly destroyed and rebuilt, on so many occasions, that there remained no certain trace of anything which might, with confidence, merit the identification.

There was, of course, no question of the location of Solomon's Temple. In the south-western corner of the Temple Mount was, and still remains, part of a surrounding wall, famous as the Wailing Wall. There is also the Dome of the Rock, at whose centre lies the sacred stone upon which, it is said, Abraham offered his son as sacrifice in obedience to God's command. This stone was acknowledged as having served as the Temple's Altar of Sacrifice. The site of Solomon's Temple was, therefore, as well known to tourists as it was to scholars. However, several options were proposed as the veritable 'Royal David's City', by topographers as well as by bible scholars and archaeologists, but the question still remained unresolved. However, the Bible provides clues.

2 Samuel - chapter 5 tells us:

> And the king and his men went to Jerusalem unto the Jebusites, the inhabitants of the land: which spake unto David, saying . . . thou shalt not come in hither: thinking, David cannot come in hither. Nevertheless, David took the strong hold of Zion: the same is the city of David. And David said on that day, Whosoever getteth up to the gutter, and smiteth the Jebusites, ... he shall be chief and captain.

1 Chronicles 11 v 6 adds to the account that : Joab the son of Zeruiah went first up, and was chief.

But, what is this 'gutter' through which Joab led the assault on the city? It is obviously a conduit of some sort. The original Hebrew text gives the word *tsinnor* which is, with rather more clarity, translated in the *New Jewish Publication Society* version as 'water shaft'. (*The Good News Bible* renders the passage as: 'go up through the water tunnel'). The Jebusite stronghold, it would seem, had a water supply, obviously outside the city walls, and to which access could be gained via a well-shaft of some kind. Joab must have led a small force in a sort of commando attack through this 'water tunnel', enabling him, it would seem, to take the defenders by surprise and to open the gates to David's waiting army.

This vital source of water can only be the 'upper watercourse' referred to in 2 Chronicles 32 v 30 when, three hundred years after David had captured the city:

> ... Hezekiah also stopped the upper watercourse of Gihon, and brought it straight down to the west side of the city of David; thus channelling the water to flow through a tunnel to a point inside the walls of Jerusalem.

Millén's 1909 expedition was the first to identify the Spring of Gihon from these descriptions. (It is now also known as 'The Virgin's Fountain' and is frequently marked as such on modern maps.) They were thus able to establish, beyond doubt, that the City of David, the veritable Mount Zion of the Jebusites, was the hill to the south of the Temple Mount. Millén and his expedition then spent some two years digging their way through the heart of the mountain and clearing Hezekiah's tunnel.

UNDERGROUND JERUSALEM.

DISCOVERIES ON THE HILL OF OPHEL (1909-11).

BY

H. V.

(of the Ecole Biblique et Archéologique in Jerusalem).

SPECIALLY TRANSLATED FROM THE FRENCH FOR THE "FIELD," AND FULLY ILLUSTRATED WITH PHOTOGRAPHS, PLANS, AND COLOURED PLATES.

LONDON:

HORACE COX,

"Field" Office, Windsor House, Bream's Buildings, E.C.

1911.

Report on the Hezekiah Tunnel by H. Vincent during Johan Millén's excavations.

Curiously, the undertaking seems to have been cloaked in a veil of security - if not absolute secrecy. The Turkish authorities, who then controlled the Holy City, provided physical protection and the expedition itself paid for an additional permanent police and military force to ensure that no unauthorised persons were allowed to approach. Without special permission, no one other than trusted

On the Right Roads, *by Johan Millén*

employees were even allowed near to the site of the excavations and this eventually, and inevitably, attracted the attention of the press. Fanciful speculations grew about Millén's true purpose, but nothing came close to the eventual revelation which he made in a small privately printed and limited-edition book published in Stockholm in 1917.

In this book, *På Rätta Vägar* (On the Right Roads), Millén admitted that while his ostensible objective was to clear the tunnel leading from the Spring of Gihon to the Pool of Siloam, his true purpose had been to search for the lost Ark of the Covenant. Was Millén a wishful-thinking fantasist? Or did he have grounds for his extraordinary and covert quest?

SECRET CODES

In his book, Millén reveals that his search was based on secret information encoded within certain books of the Old Testament - principally from the original text of the first chapter of the Book of Ezekiel. The cipher concealed within the texts had apparently been discovered by a Finn, Dr Valter Henrik Juvelius, with whom Millén had been in contact for some ten years prior to the mounting of the Parker Expedition. Millén says:

> To arrive at the concealed text, one must find the 'key' which will unlock the hidden writing. In principal, the 'key' employs letters placed by the author in special sequences, which can then be 'lifted out' and put together to form words and sentences. Needless to say, the coded messages cannot be derived from translations (of the original texts). They can only be identified in the language of the original. (*På Rätta Vägar*, p 11)

Yet again, we seem to be confronted by curious, if not dubious claims, of the sort which arouse mockery - if not downright hostility - in the academic world. However, while it is certainly true that a measure of disbelief was occasioned by a recent claim that extraordinary and prophetic ciphers have been found in the

Hebrew Old Testament texts,[43] the codes found by Dr Juvelius are of a different, and more concrete kind. They are more akin to the unquestionable Atbash cipher, described by Dr Hugh Schonfield in *Secrets of the Dead Sea Scrolls* (London 1956). In his later book, *The Essene Odyssey* (1984), Dr Schonfield convincingly demonstrates the use made of this code by the Knights Templar.[44] One is therefore treading on not altogether unfamiliar ground, with the discovery that people other than the Templars had been led underground in Jerusalem. It seems, therefore, legitimate to enquire if their impetus might not have come from some common source.

The Old Testament cipher, unravelled by Dr Juvelius, proved to be a detailed description of how the Ark of the Covenant was secreted in a hidden cavity beneath the City of David and deep inside the mountain. The cipher was supposedly encoded within the biblical texts during the sixth century BC, when the Tribe of Judah was enduring its 'Babylonian Captivity'. The Ark, it seems, had been concealed at the time of the plundering of Jerusalem by the Babylonian King Nebuchadnezzar, when the Temple was destroyed. The priests then ensured that the secret of its hiding place would be preserved for future generations, by the ingenious device of encrypting precise directions for its recovery in the otherwise opaque Book of Ezekiel.

Valter Juvelius's painstaking uncovering of the coded messages in the original texts had provided what was, in effect, a detailed treasure-map for Millén's expedition. The coded text describes an extremely complex system of underground passages, pierced through the mountain, one of which leads eventually to the cave containing the Ark of the Covenant. The entrance to the system is to be found leading off from the tunnel which links the Spring of Gihon with the Pool of Siloam.

The text is so detailed that it was possible for Millén and his team immediately to identify the Spring and to find the tunnel. This enabled them to confirm the previously uncertain location of Mount Zion. From then on, Millén assures us, the excavations were guided entirely by the detailed instructions derived from the text encoded in the Bible. His description of how the passages are constructed and how the system works makes dramatic reading:

> . . .there is a triple system of double tunnels, labyrinths and water channels, each serving a different purpose. The tunnels lead to specific sites, but the entrances are so cleverly concealed with artificial rock - which has the exact appearance of natural stone - that the way in is absolutely impossible to find without the precise guidance provided by the secret messages.
> The purpose of the labyrinths is to deviate searchers from the tunnels so that, after following various routes, they are led into an empty void.

[43] Michael Drosnin, *The Bible Code*, Weidenfeld & Nicolson, 1997.
[44] See also: *The Messianic Legacy.*

The water channels pursue different strategies, one of which is to prevent unsanctioned entry into the tunnels and labyrinths. Certain places are particularly dangerous, in that the water-channels can be (inadvertently) linked with the tunnels, causing them to flood and drowning anyone inside. As if these are not sufficient precautions against unauthorised access, there are other, equally powerful deterrents, i.e. noxious gases which can cause burning and suffocation. These vapours are produced by the material used to block the tunnels. It is only the warnings which we elicited from the secret messages encoded in the Bible texts, that prevented us from suffering serious accidents.

*The Siege of Jerusalem by Nebuchadnezzar
(18th century engraving).*

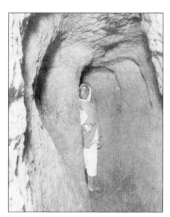

*A workman stands at the point
where the builders of Hezekiah's
tunnel met beneath the mountain.*

This description, it must be admitted, smacks of the wilder story lines of modern adventure films. However, Millén had granted unrestricted access to the site to Dr Henri Vincent, a professor at the *Ecole Biblique et Archéologique de Jérusalem*. Vincent produced a detailed report of his investigations[45] which is still acknowledged as being a most detailed, thorough and scholarly account.[46] He appears to have been more than surprised by some of the work undertaken by the teams of diggers. He recounts his great surprise when he finds them, apparently on Millén's instructions, labouring in a particular spot to dig into what appears to be the solid wall of the tunnel. In his report, he says:

> The engineers asked me to convince myself, with my own eyes and hands, that they were not cutting into the natural mountain side, but into artificial

[45] *Underground Jerusalem*, London, 1911.
[46] See QEDEM – *Monographs of the Institute of Archaeology*, The Hebrew University of Jerusalem, No 35, 1996.

rock. My doubts remained, even as I watched the tunnel increasing in breadth and depth. I took some pieces of the rock out of the tunnel and washed them in the spring. I then examined them with the aid of a magnifying glass in bright sunlight. There was absolutely no doubt that the rock was artificial. It was so hard and compact that it took considerable force to crack it.

Dr Vincent's book, is a carefully detailed physical description of the tunnels. It gives, however, little more than a rather superficial account of the activities of the Parker Expedition. He excuses this by saying:

I am committed to revealing nothing to outsiders until such time as shall be decided by the leaders of the expedition. I hope that those who feel frustrated by my silence will consider that a like discretion will be at their disposal, should I be asked to engage in a similar project at some future time.

These statements certainly provide grounds for reflection - not least of which is: are they reliable? Dr Vincent, it would certainly seem, should be accorded a degree of respect. The monograph of the Hebrew University of Jerusalem, quoted above, is dedicated to his memory and refers to him as: 'one of the pre-eminent explorers of ancient Jerusalem, whose meticulous and conscientious survey of the subterranean waterworks of the City of David between 1909 and 1911 still stands out as the most comprehensive composition on the subject'.

The Parker expedition, obviously, did not find the Ark of the Covenant. The difficulties which Millén describes meant that progress in the tunnelling had to be extremely cautious - and therefore very slow. The expedition's photographs, however, demonstrate that they had, indeed, made some seemingly important discoveries. In April 1911, after almost two years of digging, Millén called what he imagined would be a temporary halt to the work - due to lack of funds. When the expedition left the area, all traces of the secret side-passages in the Tunnel of Hezekiah were carefully re-covered and camouflaged, pending their return. However, the pause proved to be permanent.

A surviving voluminous correspondence between Millén and the authorities

A portal, discovered by the Millén expedition, deep within the mountain. Vincent's account describes it as 'the most ancient gateway of the City of David yet discovered'. It appears to mark the entrance to a subterranean 'City of David'.

substantiates his ever more anxious, but eventually fruitless, attempts to gain permission for the resumption of the work. The outbreak of the First World War in 1914 compounded the difficulties and, after the war, the political climate had completely changed. The Turkish authorities with whom he had been dealing were no longer in control of Jerusalem. The British now held the reins and Millén's attempts to return to his search proved fruitless. He was never able to complete his undertaking. The frustration left him embittered and angry and led to his eventual decision to publish at least something of the true nature of his quest.

His book, *På Rätta Vägar,* however, reached only a very limited public and was never translated out of Swedish. Moreover, it is more than likely that the majority of even those few to whom it became accessible may have considered his account to be too fanciful to be true. But there was one person who thought the information worth pursuing. This was a Swedish engineer, Henry Kjellson, who stumbled upon Millén's book in 1922, five years after its publication. Kjellson found the suggestion of secret information concealed within the Old Testament to be of sufficient interest that he made a determined effort to verify the claim.

It was after many years of research that Kjellson finally succeeded in tracking down a number of letters, written to Millén by Dr Juvelius, the discoverer of the ciphers. In the letters, Juvelius describes the traps which await the unwary searcher who attempts to force a way into the system of tunnels. Kjellson published some of this material in 1961, in a book entitled *Försvunden Teknik* (Vanished Technology).[47] But it would seem extremely unlikely that some of the traps which are described, could have been created almost three thousand years ago. One of them even appears to involve the use of radioactive material.

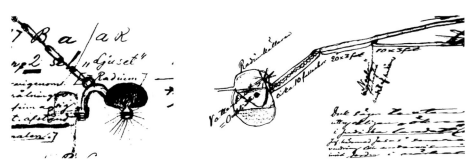

Scribbled notes by Henrik Juvelius.
They show his cipher workings, as well as the sketch of the 'radioactive' trap.

Juvelius writes in detail about this extraordinary stratagem. It is a large and heavy lump of lead, fashioned with a hollow space to contain one half of an hour-glass-shaped receptacle, so that the other half is exposed. The hour-glass is filled with a substance described as 'radioactive sand'. The lead container is attached to

[47] Henry Kjellson, *Försvunden Teknik.* 1961 - republished Valentin Forlag, Stockholm, 1995.

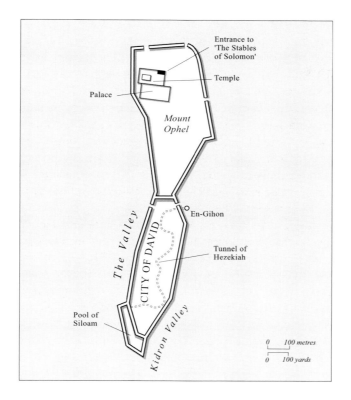

a spike and so balanced that the uncovered part of the hour-glass is to the bottom. Thus the 'radioactive sand' is exposed in the visible lower portion of the hour-glass and is emitting deadly radiation into the cave where it is placed. A chain is attached, which makes it possible, from a 'protected' position outside the cave, to invert the lead container and allow the sand to run back into the protected portion of the hour-glass. In this way, the radiation is blocked and the environment of the cave is rendered harmless.

Kjellson was able, finally, to track down a daughter of Juvelius and in 1960 obtained the details of the cipher which had apparently unravelled these extraordinary hidden messages in the Old Testament. But, apart from confirming the details provided by Millén's 1917 publication, his book goes no further into the problem. Kjellson was planning a follow-up based upon his own researches, but within a matter of months of receiving the new material, he was dead and the matter remained unresolved.

Certainly, however, these tales verge on the incredible. It is very difficult to accept them at face value. Nevertheless, there is at least one tangible piece of evidence which cannot be disputed, but can only be properly understood if we grant to the inhabitants of the Jerusalem of three thousand years ago, a scientific skill and knowledge which can only be described as 'modern'. This evidence relates directly to Hezekiah's construction of the water-tunnel which leads from the Spring of Gihon to the Pool of Siloam. The tunnel is still there to be seen and touched. Tourists to Jerusalem may enter it and admire the skill with which it was constructed. Even today, one is impressed by the achievement of Hezekiah's workmen, who were able to bore their way through the solid rock of the mountain, leaving an absolutely level floor, on a constant and even slope, in order to ensure the smooth flowing of the water. The difference in height between the two ends is no more than thirty centimetres. This has been achieved even though the tunnel does not, as one might expect, cut directly through the mountain, but instead follows a long - and apparently haphazard - meandering path. This winding course is difficult to explain. It has been suggested that the reason lay in the necessity to avoid disturbing the Tomb of King David. This suggestion, in itself, presupposes an impressive ability to survey and measure the route.

The Hebrew University's monograph of 1996 describes the system as 'among the most impressive engineering accomplishments of the biblical period.' It also refers to aspects of the work which 'have puzzled scholars ever since the waterworks were rediscovered in the mid-19th century, and many attempts have been made to account for them.' Dan Gill, author of the monograph, proposes as his explanation that the waterworks could have been 'fashioned along the pre-existing tracks of a natural ... system of shafts and conduits'. This would, of course, account for the choice of such an apparently wayward course. However, arguments have been raised against Gill's hypothesis, stemming from the extreme impermeability of rock. The problem is further compounded by an inscription carved into the wall of the tunnel by the original constructors in the days of King Hezekiah.

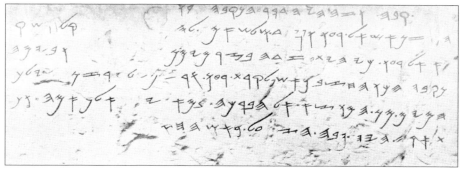

The inscription in Hezekiah's Tunnel, which marks the spot where the two teams of diggers met. (The stone is now in Istanbul.)

The text reads:

> Behold this tunnel! This has been the history of its construction: While the stonemasons still lifted their pickaxes into the air, each against his opposite neighbour, and while there were still three cubits to cut through, each could hear the voice of the other, shouting to his opposite neighbour, while there was still remaining mountain both to left and to right. And on the day of the breakthrough, they picked to meet their opposite neighbour, pickaxe against pickaxe, and the water was running from the Spring to the Pool, twelve hundred cubits and the mountain above the workers was one hundred cubits high.

If the seemingly reasonable explanation for the course of the waterway is accepted, one must wonder why Hezekiah deemed it necessary to undertake the enormous labour of enlarging it? The inscription makes the clear implication that the tunnel was cut by two teams, one working downwards from the Spring, the other upwards from the Pool. Each team followed a twisting course and yet they were able to maintain a constant slope and still meet at a presumably prearranged spot in the depth of the mountain. If they were not following pre-existent conduits, then the surveying skills and meticulous planning demonstrated by such a remarkable feat would be truly astonishing. Even today, with all the aids of modern technology, it would not be at all an easy task. The modern engineer, with the most up-to-date and sophisticated equipment, would certainly find it possible - but still, unquestionably, a challenging undertaking.

In addition, there remains yet another apparently insignificant detail of Hezekiah's tunnel which must be considered. In the context of the surveying skills revealed by the landscape configurations of Bornholm and Rennes-le-Château and the intriguing 'coincidence' of Jerusalem lying at two thousand English miles from each place, this oddity assumes an unexpected importance.

The length of the tunnel is specified in the wall inscription as twelve hundred cubits. The fact that the trouble was taken to record the length, allied to the fact that 1200 was considered a sacred number could, perhaps, suggest that the measure was intended. If this is, indeed, the case, then here may be another explanation for the apparently random contortions of the chosen path which was equally clearly pre-decided. The meanders ensure that the tunnel achieves its final and necessary length. That length has now, of course, been re-measured. It proves to be 512.50 metres. Here, then, is an opportunity to confirm the length of the Jewish Sacred Cubit. 512.5 ÷1200 = 0.427m. This is equal to 1.4 feet or one foot four and eight tenths inches.

These measures appear to be unexceptional - and why should they be anything else? But, in fact, we are looking at a truly astonishing example of the lost knowledge which we have been teasing out from the obscurity surrounding the remarkable activities of the Templars and those other shadowy figures who delved beneath Jerusalem and left their traces on Bornholm and at Rennes-le-Château.

One of the most fascinating aspects of the measure systems used in both latter places, has been the appearance of the English measure. And here, in Hezekiah's Tunnel in Jerusalem, the English units appear yet again: 1200 cubits of length 1.4 feet = 1680 feet – and that measure, multiplied by the ancient pi of twenty-two sevenths gives: 1680 x 22 ÷ 7 = 5280 feet.

The sacred number of 1200 Jewish cubits measures the diameter of a circle whose circumference is precisely one English mile.

Nor should it be forgotten that a link to the mile, is also a link to the dimensions of the Earth. In addition, the English foot can be shown to relate very simply and precisely to the Jewish Sacred Cubit. That relationship is exactly seven fifths. If the Sacred Cubit of 1.4 feet is divided into seven parts, then each part will measure 0.2, or one fifth, of a foot. And five such units are, of course, equal to one foot.

As postscript to this section, it is also worthy of comment that the distance from

16th century engraving of the Ark of the Covenant.

the Gihon Spring, across the Kidron Valley to the original location of the Ark of the Covenant on the Temple Mount, seems to be this same significant distance of 1200 cubits. There is, perhaps, another 'unlikely coincidence' to be wrung from this fact.

Did the Templars, too, find an unknown subterranean City of David during their nine years of burrowing? Is there a labyrinth of tunnels, as Millén believed, that pierces the ground beneath the Temple Mount, to cross the Kidron Valley to the Spring? Curious that in the first Grail story, the principal character bears the name Perceval ... the Piercer of the Valley.

Part Three
PROOFS

… when you have eliminated the impossible
whatever remains, however improbable,
must be the truth.

Sherlock Holmes
'The Valley of Fear'
Sir Arthur Conan Doyle

Chapter Eight
MILES & CUBITS

With the English mile measure making its reappearance in the Tunnel of Hezekiah, we are once again turned back to the heart of the mystery. Bornholm has shown us the beginnings of the complexity of its layout. But there is much more to learn before we can grope towards an understanding of what the creators of the island's geometry are trying to say to us.

Already the layout has made the unlooked-for link with the English mile and has used its ingenious structure to demonstrate a profound knowledge of nature. Yet there seems to be no obvious sign of the English measure in any ancient system which has left identifiable traces. Here, then, is the next path to be followed through the labyrinth. Where may the links reveal themselves? There is no surprise in finding that the signposts seem to lead along a well-trodden track. There is a remarkable and indisputable proof of a relationship between the English pole and the Ancient Egyptian Royal Cubit.

The relationship is a simple, though not obvious one. The Royal Cubit has been defined as 20.625 inches.[48] This is an exact fraction of a mile. 63360 inches divided by 20.625 = 3072.

Here, again, are the same basic factors which make the divisions simple. 3072 is 3 multiplied by 2^{10} (two multiplied by itself ten times). As is shown in the Table on page 74 above, this number is 'practical'. It can be broken down into the same basic factors.

> The pole = 198 inches (2 x 3 x 3 x 11)
> 198 x 5 ÷ 2 ÷ 2 ÷ 2 ÷ 2 ÷ 3 = 20.625

This relationship between the pole and the Egyptian Royal Cubit arises from the fact that both are derived from the same measurement of the earth. Exactly the same measurement. The evidence for this is to be found in the dimensions of the Great Pyramid.

It is noteworthy that, at the end of the nineteenth century, the Great Pyramid was used as an important scientific proof that there had been no alteration in the earth's poles. The age of the Great Pyramid has been the subject of debate for

---

[48] William Matthew Flinders Petrie, *The Great Pyramid*, London 1893.

centuries - and even more so today. It would seem that the Pyramid dates back at least four millennia; some researchers maintain that it is considerably older. It is oriented today, (as it presumably was when built), to face with great precision due north, south, east and west. This would seem to confirm that this orientation does not change over millennia. (Modern geophysics has been able to verify this fact.) But it is not only the orientation of the Great Pyramid which demonstrates extreme accuracy. To the great surprise of historians, there is a very precise pi-relationship between the Pyramid's height and its circumference.

As with the establishment of its age, there is also some difficulty in calculating the exact height of the Great Pyramid. The uncertainty arises, as the cap-stone is now missing. There is, of course, a straightforward mathematical solution to the problem. It is possible to calculate, with complete accuracy, the theoretical angle of the rising side, if we assume an exact pi-relationship between base and height. The angle defined by this relationship would then be 51° 51' 14.3".

On the north side of the Pyramid, archaeologists have excavated intact carved stones which have made it possible to calculate the angle very precisely. Numerous measurements at varying locations have established a mean of 51° 51' 14". Here is proof that the builders were aware of, and used, a pi-relationship which was accurate to at least four decimal places. This is so amazing that historians still find great difficulty in accepting the fact. But there is yet one more thing, apparently hitherto overlooked, which can be deduced from this pi-relationship. And it is no less surprising.

With the pi-relationship between height and base established, it is possible to calculate the Pyramid's original height simply by dividing half the circumference of the base by pi. Of the numerous attempts which have been made to produce accurate measurements, the present study will be based upon the work of Flinders Petrie, which was carried out at the end of the nineteenth century.[49] His survey seems to be the most reliable as it was not only meticulous, but was completed before later excavations introduced the risk of compromising the reliability of the present placing of the corner stones.

The lay-out of the base proves to be surprisingly accurate, though with tiny discrepancies. Flinders Petrie gives the following dimensions for the four sides:

North	:	230.25 metres	(755.41 feet)
South	:	230.45 metres	(756.07 feet)
East	:	230.39 metres	(755.87 feet)
West	:	230.36 metres	(755.77 feet)

With such a small variation, (the twenty centimetres difference between the longest and the shortest sides is equal to barely 8 inches), it would seem obvious that a specific measure must have been intended.

[49] William Matthew Flinders Petrie, *op cit*

In order to establish what this measure might have been, the Danish architect Hubert Paulsen turned to a text in the Temple of the Sun of the Fifth Dynasty Pharaoh Neuserre (c 2400 BC). This inscription describes how the goddess Seshat had helped the king in the laying out of his temple. According to the text, the goddess specifies that the central axis - that which runs from north to south - is to be fixed before the sides are laid out.

Using this technique, Paulsen measured the central axis of the Great Pyramid, which he found to be 230.375 metres (755.82 feet). This, then, was presumably the intended length of the sides. The ideal circumference of the pyramid's base is therefore four times 230.375 = 921.5 metres. Using the established pi-relationship, it is now possible to calculate the height of the pyramid: 921.5 : pi : 2 = 146.66 metres.

It seems not to have been noticed that this is a truly astonishing result.

Egyptologists have determined that each side of the Great Pyramid's base should have a length of 440 Royal Cubits. It would appear that nobody has recognised that the height is also expressed in 440 units - though of a different measure. With the cap-stone missing, it had been necessary to reconstruct the height by calculation, which is the probable reason why this important observation had been missed. It seems that the height of the pyramid is not to be defined by the length of its base. The calculation must have been performed the other way round. In other words, there must have been a predetermined required height for the Pyramid and it is this measure which determines the length of the base.

That the Royal Cubit is defined by the height of the Great Pyramid, can be demonstrated. The above calculations have fixed the original height as 146.66 metres. If this measure is divided into 440 equal parts, the basic measurement proves to be 0.3333 metres - an exact one third of our present metre. This means that the height of the Pyramid is defined by a unit derived from the measurement of the earth's polar circumference.

The Pyramid builders, however, did not use the division of forty million, which results in our present metre. Instead, they divided the circumference into 120 million equal parts - each being one third of a metre in length. 120 - ten times twelve - is much more in accord with ancient systems of measure. But there remains yet one more important piece of evidence.

The metre-reference system which is used to divide the earth's polar circumference is quadragesimal - based upon a square division. The pyramid system, however, is hexagesimal - i.e. it is based upon a one sixth division of the polar circumference. The very position of the Great Pyramid is proof of this suggestion. As viewed from the centre of the earth, the angle between the north pole and the Pyramid is sixty degrees. With extreme accuracy, the Pyramid lies on the tip of a hexagon oriented upon and inscribed within the polar circumference.

Figure 15

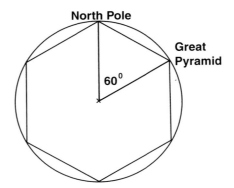

A measurement of sixty degrees from the north pole would place the Great Pyramid at the latitude of exactly thirty degrees. Its geographical latitude is presently given as 29° 58' 51.06''. At slightly less than two kilometres, (one and a quarter miles), from the exact thirty degree latitude, this is impressively accurate. Given that there are several different methods for calculating latitude, the one chosen by the pyramid builders might even account for this discrepancy.

The polar circumference of the earth defines the measure used to determine the height of the Pyramid and, given the pi-relationship between height and base, the same measure determines the length of the Royal Cubit. According to the Egyptologists, the base of the Pyramid is circumscribed by four times 440 - i.e. 1760 - Royal Cubits. There are also 1760 yards in an English mile. Both the English and the Pyramid measure system are developed using factors of two, five and eleven.

It is the factor eleven which demonstrates the relationship between the two systems, rather as modern gene technology can be used to establish family relationships between apparently unconnected individuals. The factor eleven is the 'distinguishing gene' which proves the intimate link.

The above calculations lead us to suggest that the 'one-third metre' measure should be regarded as the true basic measurement of the Ancient Egyptians and that it was from this unit that their cubit and remen measures were derived. The remen has a square-root two relationship to the cubit; and the cubit has a pi-relationship to the 'one-third metre' measure. It can, perhaps, be looked upon as the 'Sacred Metre' of Ancient Egypt. It is possible that this Sacred Metre was kept as a reference - just as a platinum metre was once preserved in Paris.

Certainly, as we have already shown, the French scientists who defined that metre in the eighteenth century would have achieved better results if they had used the English pole. They could equally well have defined it by dividing the Egyptian Royal Cubit by twenty-two sevenths and multiplying the result by six.

THE TOISE & THE TEMPLARS

It is fascinating to discover that the French even had a native measure which they could have used. Their antique toise proves also to be based upon a precise measure of the earth's polar circumference.

The *toise* is equal to 1.96 metres. There seems, at first, to be no obvious connection. But, interestingly, when expressed as a fraction, 1.96 is the equivalent of forty nine twenty fifths (49 ÷ 25 = 1.96). 49 is 7 x 7 - and 25 is 5 x 5. $7^2 \div 5^2$ = 1.96. Here is an altogether felicitous link between *toise* and metre. Or should it still be argued that nothing but blind coincidence is at work?

There is, furthermore, a subtle and extremely practical link between the toise and its unnoticed derivation. This has to do with the construction of the regular octagon. Suddenly, the shadow of the Knights Templar can be sensed at the edge of our vision, for the octagon was frequently employed in Templar architecture.

The relationship between the radius and the side of a regular octagon is extremely complicated. (To define the side, one must multiply the radius by the square-root of (two minus square-root two)). Such a calculation would be almost impossibly difficult to explain to an uneducated workforce, and how, indeed, could they be expected to perform it? The desired mathematical operation is, however, remarkably simple to achieve if the *toise* measure is used to define the radius of the octagon and the metre is used to define the side.

With a radius of one *toise*, an octagon's circumference will measure exactly 12 metres.

A comparison with the Royal Cubit is inescapable.

With a radius of one metre, the circumference will measure 12 Royal Cubits.

The ancient measure systems do, indeed, seem to be linked in curious - if familiar - ways.

Just as with the English measure system, the *toise* provides another simple and efficient way to work with an irrational number. This time, it is the fraction forty-nine twenty-fifths which gives a practical relationship between the side and the radius of a regular octagon:

With radius equal to one toise, 49 : 25 (or 1.96) x √ (2 - √2) x 8 gives the circumference of the octagon.

The exact circumference is 12.000952 metres - just under one millimetre too long, but accurate enough for practical use.

There is, of course, another practicality. It is very easy to calculate the square-root of the above fraction. It is 7 : 5.

This inter-play of apparently different units of measure may explain why Egyptologists have remarked that the length of the Royal Cubit is slightly larger than the cubit which may be deduced from the base of the Great Pyramid. The apparent anomaly will be explicable if we take the Pyramid to be constructed using a more accurate pi as the link between the 'Sacred Metre' and the cubit. For practical, day-to-day usage, the link between the Sacred Metre and the Royal Cubit would be the simpler pi - i.e. twenty-two sevenths.

If the real unchangeable reference is the Sacred Metre, then the Royal Cubit, (derived from a pi equal to twenty-two sevenths), will be slightly larger than the Royal Cubit in the base of the Pyramid, which is derived from a pi accurate to four decimal places.

In passing, it is worth noting that the *toise* is also equal to an old Spanish measure, the *gizabethe*. This was divided into seven *pie* - three of which were equal to a *vara*. The length of the Spanish *vara* (0.84 metres) is thus also related to a precise division of the earth's polar circumference.

It would be possible to continue describing antique systems of measure and their fascinating inter-relationships both with each other and with the circumference of the earth. However, it is not the purpose of this book to make an in-depth analysis of this rather abstruse subject, but merely to draw attention to the existence of a basic and universal measure, which is easily to be found in ancient systems once the key has been identified.

The non-mathematically minded reader may have found some of the above explanations confusing and difficult to comprehend. Nevertheless, we feel that they may have served the purpose of opening yet another portal into the shadowy accounts of the actions and knowledge of the creators of our basic puzzle. They may also serve to strengthen the question of why on earth (!) the modern world has rejected the older and more accurate - as well as more practical - units in favour of the metre and its attendant irrational calculations.

Chapter Nine
EXPLORATION
OF THE CIRCLE

Bornholm is a mathematical and geometrical treasure house. For the knowledgeable mathematician, the co-ordinates listed later in this book are all that is now necessary to embark upon a voyage of discovery. The geometry, with all its skilful use of number, proportion and angle, will reveal itself in ever more fascinating and complex layers.

In Chapters Four and Five above, we have described in a simplified manner the basic patterns which have appeared. We must now explore some of these in rather more detail, as they will show us how to unravel some unexpected additional discoveries, some of which will exhibit a particularly impressive ingenuity. They will demonstrate extremely clever methods for solving age-old mathematical problems. But first we must return to the last of the star-shapes which we have examined.

The pentagram was subtly hidden on Bornholm, with its centre fixed upon a seemingly empty spot which we have labelled P2 (see Figure 14, page 66). This location, unmarked by any church, will lead into the heart of the message which has been spread across the island. We are approaching the spider which is patiently waiting at the centre of its web.

This last part of the geometry is concerned, not with star-shapes, but with the Circle. Specifically, it is the first of the circles to which attention was drawn. The circle whose radius is defined by the island's basic unit of measure: the distance between the centres of the circular churches of Østerlars and Nylars. The circumference of this prime circle will prove to have a most instructive lesson to impart. The description which follows may appear complex to the non-mathematician, but is, in reality, made up of a sequence of simple and logical steps.

In Figure 14 (p 66), the centre of the five-pointed star, (designated P2), can be seen to lie on the point where the Østerlars/Nylars line intersects with the line which connects Knudsker with Ibsker. This location controls the placing of Ibsker with absolute precision.

As can be seen in Figure 11 (p 60), Ibsker is so placed that the distance from Østerlars to Ibsker is exactly the same as the distance between the round churches of Olsker and Nyker. This distance, which is meticulously indicated by the

Knudsker church is dedicated to the Danish King Knud den Hellige, who was murdered in 1086. He was beatified in 1100 and is buried in St Knud's church, Odense.

Geometrical Key, also defines the radius of the circle which is inscribed within the square-root seven triangle, (see Figure 12 p. 60). Ibsker is, of course, on the circumference of this circle and its position is not random. The hidden five-pointed star provides an exact definition of Ibsker's place in the design.

Figure 14 (p.66) shows how Ibsker helps to define P2, the centre of the pentagram. Its exact relationship with the geometry, however, appears to be uncertain. Figure 16 on page 117 shows that the position is, in fact, elegantly chosen. It marks the intersection of two circles – the first placed upon P2, the second on Østerlars. The particularly significant detail is the precise distance of Ibsker from P2 which relates directly to the circumference of the original prime Østerlars circle. It can be shown to be a demonstration of a geometrical method for the calculation of the circumference.

This – as with so many of these seemingly complex matters - requires a brief explanation for the reader unversed in the basic mathematics. The length of a circle's circumference is slightly more than three times its diameter. The exact relationship of circumference and diameter cannot, however, be expressed by a rational number, which can define only an approximation. Here, again, we confront pi and its inexact equivalent of twenty-two sevenths.

The beautifully painted central pillar of Nylars church. These are the oldest of the frescos on Bornholm, executed at, or very shortly after, the construction of the church.

King Charles XIII of Sweden in his regalia as Grand Master of Swedish Freemasonry. Behind him is the red cross of the Knights Templar.

A 19th century engraving of a Knight Templar.

Knights in crusaders' chain mail in Østerlars church.

The Lamb of God sheds its blood into the Holy Grail. (Nyker church).

Figure 16

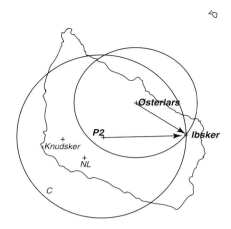

We have demonstrated in Chapter 6 above, that the ancients used this rough but practical definition. (Twenty-two sevenths equal 3.142857..... A more exact pi would be 3.1415926.....) For the large majority of practical calculations, 22/7 would provide sufficient accuracy, but occasionally a more refined definition was required. This was a constant challenge to mathematicians, throughout history. How, by use of compasses and straightedge alone, to construct the relationship between diameter and circumference? That is – how to use the diameter to produce the length of the circumference *as a straight line?* The next step in the geometry of Bornholm demonstrates an ingenious response to this problem.

The distance from P2 to Ibsker proves to be, with total accuracy, an exact one sixth of the original Østerlars / Nylars circle circumference. Thus, schematically, it should be possible to fix Ibsker's position on the inscribed 'square root seven' circle by simply setting a pair of compasses to one sixth of the Østerlars circumference and then drawing an arc centred on P2. The intersection of arc and 'square root seven' circle would then establish Ibsker's position.

This mathematically controlled point lies within the apse of the mediaeval church, just to the west of the altar. Once more, the placing of the church seems to have been calculated with extreme care.

However, there is one major difficulty to be found in carrying out the above, apparently straightforward, instructions. It is simply not possible to set a pair of compasses to an exact one sixth of a circumference. The compasses can only measure the length of a straight line, not the curved length of an arc. The calculation of the sixth of a circumference, with the accuracy exhibited on Bornholm was, supposedly, impossible for a mediaeval mathematician. Unless, of course, the devisers of this system were in possession of information, methods and skills which have, hitherto, remained unrecognised.

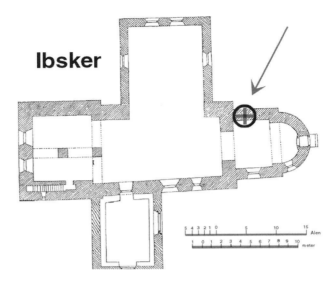

Figure 17

Again we seem to be confronting secret and privileged knowledge, guarded *solis sacerdotibus,* 'only for the initiated'. For the devisers of the layout certainly possessed this knowledge. Moreover, on Bornholm they demonstrate their method. It is simply built into the geometry. We are looking at a teaching aid – a geometrical textbook - from which the student, once he has been taught how to open the pages, can learn skills unimagined by the world in which his teachers lived.

The message is hidden in the line from Knudsker to Ibsker. This is the line which intersects the Østerlars / Nylars axis at P2, the centre of the hidden pentagram. This line has several interesting properties. For example, its length is precisely one fourth of the circumference of the basic Østerlars circle. The line, itself, explains how this was achieved.

There is a ridge which runs across the middle of the island. Where the Knudsker / Ibsker line crosses this ridge is, interestingly enough, the highest point on Bornholm. We have designated this point as P1. Looking north-westwards from this point, it is possible to see the spire of Klemensker church. Beyond, and directly behind Klemensker is the spire of Rutsker church. Thus, it can clearly be seen that P1 is the intersection of the Knudsker / Ibsker line and a prolongation of the line through Rutsker and Klemensker.

Just as P1 is placed to mark the highest point on Bornholm's ridge, the churches of Rutsker and Klemensker are also set upon high spots in the landscape. It seems, therefore, that the natural topography of the landscape must have been taken into account by whoever laid out the design. The landscape relief must have been carefully plotted and taken into account in the very earliest stages of the planning. Even so, this

Figure 18

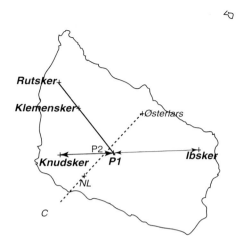

fact has been hidden until this late stage in the investigation. The impression is gained that till now we have been slowly working our way across the web. Now we can sense that we are approaching the centre where the spider lies in wait.

Klemensker – (St Clement's church).   *Rutsker.*

Both churches dominate the landscape from their gentle hilltops. Rutsker was originally dedicated to St Michael – saint of the high places. Rutsker is, in fact, the highest positioned church in Denmark.

DIVINE PROPORTION

P1 has been defined as the intersection of two lines: Knudsker / Ibsker and Rutsker / Klemensker. But it is more than this. P1 divides the Knudsker / Ibsker line in exact Golden Section proportion - 1 : 1.618. Again, we are confronting that magical number, inherent in the pentagram and which, in Professor Cornford's words, 'excited awe and reverence'. Here is the detail which unlocks the hidden, secret message.

The distance from Knudsker to P1 proves to be the exact three fifths of the basic Østerlars / Nylars unit. **(15680 yards ÷ 5 x 3 = 9408 yards)**
Since P1 also divides the line in Golden Section proportion,
it follows that the remainder of the line – P1 to Ibsker – must be that three fifths division, multiplied by the Golden Section.
(9408 x 1.6180339 = 15222.4629312)
Therefore, the distance from Knudsker to Ibsker is:
 15222.4629312 + 9408 = 24630.4629312 yards.
Further : as the entire Knudsker / Ibsker line has proved to be one fourth of the basic circle's circumference (see above), then this calculation demonstrates a method for the computation of the circumference by use of three fifths and the Golden Proportion.

Those readers who wish to verify the details with their pocket calculators, will find the following clear confirmation of Bornholm's use of the 'secret Golden Section-based pi'.

The radius of the Østerlars / Nylars circle has been theoretically established as **15680 yards.**
Using the ancient pi of 22/7, the circumference is
2 (15680 x 22 ÷ 7) = 98560 yards or exactly 56 English miles.

However, by using the more accurate pi, the circumference can be calculated with greater precision.

2 x 15680 x 3.141592654 = 98520.34562 yards.
The difference (98560 – 98520.34562) is **39.654834 yards.**
This demonstrates that 22/7 is not an exact pi-relation.

The calculation should now be again performed, but using the ancient Golden Section 'secret pi-approximation'.

The Knudsker / Ibsker line, defined above, measures
24630.4629312 yards.
It is equal to one fourth of the circumference.
Therefore, the circumference is
24630.4629312 x 4 = 98521.85172 yards.
The difference from the exact pi-calculation is:
98521.8517248 - 98520.34562 = 1.5061 yards.

The discrepancy has reduced from nearly forty yards to one and a half yards. **This is a mere fifty-four inches over a measured distance of fifty-six miles ... less than one inch in 63360.**

This simple Golden Section calculation can, indeed, be looked upon as a magical formula for which mathematicians had been searching for many centuries.

And there remains one more crucial element in this Bornholm method which will be more impressive to the mathematician than to the general reader:

Unlike our present exact pi, this very accurate 'Golden Section-based pi' can be constructed as a straight line, solely by use of compass and straight edge.

The first European mathematician to produce a construction with a comparable accuracy was A.A. Kotjanski, in 1685[50]. His method is different – and is less accurate. This implies that the Bornholm construction was not generally known to mathematicians in the outside world and must have been reserved as privileged and secret information.

The division on the Knudsker / Ibsker line, indicated by P1 is an excellent confirmation of the teaching intent of the geometric layout. Without it, the significance of the P2 to Ibsker distance would probably never have been recognised.

Figure 19 below shows how the distance from Knudsker to Ibsker is divided by P1, so that, with Østerlars / Nylars as the basic unit, the two parts are of length three fifths and three fifths multiplied by the Golden Section. The sum of the two parts is equal to one fourth of the circle circumference.

Figure 19

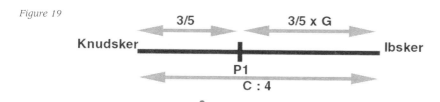

The following diagram shows that P2 divides the line into the proportions of one twelfth and one sixth of the circle's circumference.

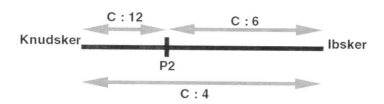

[50] Petr Beckmann *A history of Pi*, New York 1971

The third diagram demonstrates how the P2 division makes it possible to rediscover how one fifth of the unit length, in interaction with the Golden Section, can express different portions of the circle's circumference.

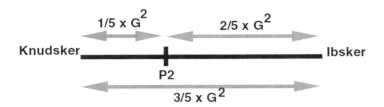

While the numbers may give the appearance of complexity, they are essentially simple. All that is needed are the one fifth division of the line and the square of the Golden Section. As was pointed out on page 65 above, to multiply the Golden Section by itself, it is only necessary to add one. **(1.6180339 x 1.6180339 = 2.6180339).** As noted in the calculations above, the three fifths division is 9408 yards.

9408 x 2.6180339 = 24630.4629312.

The lengths of the lines are equal to the equivalent circle arcs to a level of extreme accuracy. The difference, for example, of the one twelfth arc of the circumference from the equivalent one twelfth division of the line is as little as 0.000008 – i.e. less than one hundred thousandth.

In these latter steps, we have uncovered subtle and ingenious calculations which have survived as a well-guarded secret since the Middle Ages.

Figure 20

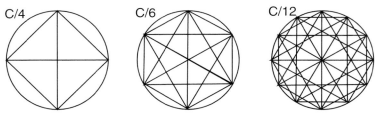

As this Figure shows, the one fourth, one sixth and one twelfth divisions of a circle's circumference are precisely those most commonly used in the symbols of sacred geometry. They define the inscribed square; the hexagram (Star of David or Seal of Solomon); and the dodecagram which is also frequently used in Christian sacred symbolism.

But we have not yet reached the heart of Bornholm's geometry. The greatest of all its secrets have yet to be revealed. As we approach the centre of the web, a treasure still remains to be uncovered.

GENIUS UNLOCKED

To find the pathway to the very centre of this spider's web, it is necessary to turn outwards yet again. It is the circumference of the circle which encloses the secret. Before approaching the most extraordinary of all the revelations of Bornholm, there still remains one example of mathematical dexterity to uncover. How was it possible to place the church of Klemensker, with nearly perfect precision, upon the point of a seven-sided star?

This undertaking is far from straightforward, as the seven-pointed heptagon is one of those geometric figures which cannot be constructed by the simple use of straight-edge and compasses. Yet again, the layout reveals a most ingenious method by which this seemingly impossible task can be achieved.

> The church of Rutsker is so placed on the main circle's circumference, that the angle which it forms with the round churches of Østerlars and Nylars is sixty-nine degrees. (This is an angle which can be constructed by use of a pair of compasses.)[51]
>
> A line is then drawn to connect Rutsker and P1.
>
> This line will intersect the inner circle at one seventh of its circumference from the main axis – i.e. the vertex of the heptagon, marked by Klemensker church.

Figure 21

---

[51] The square, the pentagon and the hexagon *can*, of course be simply constructed. The square produces 90°, from which can be subtracted the 72° of the pentagram. The resulting 18° can be divided into two and this 9° added to the hexagon's 60°.

This intersection is, in fact, an approximation, but its accuracy is such that when the colossal star-figure is laid out on the Bornholm landscape, the point is displaced by no more than two and a half metres.

When one is reminded that these churches have stood on their pre-ordained and carefully plotted positions for nearly a thousand years, one must wonder whence came this stunning expertise. Centuries were to pass before our civilisation became openly capable of like feats.

Why had it been necessary to hide so glowing a light beneath so opaque a bushel? Perhaps it was the obduracy of the Church, such as was experienced by Galileo, that bred a caution which would be, to us, incomprehensible. It should be remembered that the Templars were involved in this work. Their fate, with its accusations of heresy and worship of the devil, may hint at the reason. In their world, so alien to us, such knowledge trailed the scent of the sulphur of hell-fire. Certainly, there would have been an over-riding need for secrecy.

What then remains for the Bornholm builders to teach us? What does the spider guard at the heart of its web?

At the beginning of this investigation, it seemed that Østerlars, the largest, most beautiful and most impressive of the churches, would lie at the centre of the mystery. But the layout has proved cleverer and more subtle than this. With the discovery of the centre of the pentagram, P2, and the very clear indication of P1, the island's highest point, we have struggled towards what must have been the very first spot to be fixed in the layout.

The next, and final, step discloses *why* the geometry is structured around P1 and P2. This revelation becomes apparent when the last of the churches, Povlsker, is assigned its place in the geometry.

Povlsker is so placed that its distance from P1 is the same as the distance from P1 to Ibsker. It is also positioned so that its distance from Ibsker is exactly half of the distance between Ibsker and Knudsker.

Figure 22

124

With Povlsker's position thus accurately defined, it must now be observed, not from P1, but from P2.

Figure 23

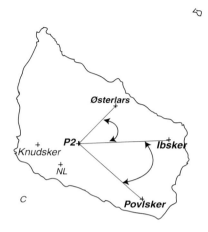

P2 shows two adjacent angles. The first is formed with Østerlars and Ibsker; the second with Ibsker and Povlsker. The first angle is slightly larger than the second. With a pair of compasses, it is a simple matter to subtract the smaller angle from the larger.

The tiny and apparently insignificant residue is no less than a geometrical sensation.

Povlsker, (St Paul's church).

Ibsker, (St James's church – 'Ib' is Jacob or James).

These two churches are interlocked with precision, relative to one of the crucial geometric points.

Povlsker church shows clear traces of the influence of the gothic and is considered to be the last of the mediaeval churches to be built on Bornholm. As Povlsker demonstrates the final goal of the geometry, the late dating provides possible confirmatory evidence.

SOLUTION TO AN ANCIENT PROBLEM

The mathematicians of antiquity struggled with three famous and knotty problems. The first is at least known to, if not properly understood by, most people: the Squaring of the Circle. We all know it as one of those 'impossibilities', which we can use in a metaphorical sense without fully grasping its mathematical import, which is to construct a square equal in area to a given circle.

The second problem is the Duplication of the Cube – how to construct a cube with twice the volume of another given cube. Yet another puzzle which cannot be solved by use of ruler and compasses.

The third great problem is the Trisection of the Angle. While this may seem astonishing to the non-mathematician, the division of an arbitrary angle into three, using only straightedge and compasses, is impossible to achieve. The attempt exercised such great minds as René Descartes in the seventeenth century, yet the Bornholm builders had provided an ingenious solution five hundred years before.

The tiny portion left over by the subtraction of the angle at P2 proves to measure, with incredible accuracy, sixteen ninths of a degree. This means that, by further division of this angle it is possible to construct one ninth of a degree.

$$16 \div 2 = 8$$
$$8 \div 2 = 4$$
$$4 \div 2 = 2$$
$$2 \div 2 = 1$$

The mathematically untutored among us may wonder why such an apparently dull game with numbers can be termed 'a sensation'. But such it is.

Although matters of this kind may seem to impinge little on the lives of most of us, even so, we can dimly grasp that incredibly complex calculations must have been necessary in order, for example, to send astronauts on their intrepid missions into space. The ability to conjure with numbers is built invisibly into the very fabric of our existence. To find that our forefathers of a millennium past were, in their way, as skilled as we, is astonishing.

The mathematician will understand completely why the construction of one ninth of a degree is a brilliant feat. Three degrees is the smallest angle that can be constructed in whole degrees – and it has been proven impossible, by ruler and compasses, to divide an angle into three parts. Therefore, it is not possible to construct an angle of one degree. Neither is it possible to construct one third of a degree. And of course, it is likewise impossible to construct an angle of one ninth of a degree. But Bornholm has just demonstrated how to achieve the impossible.

Since it is a simple matter to *add* three angles, we can now, from one ninth of a degree construct one third of a degree. And three such angles will give the 'impossible' one degree.

Let us immediately state that the Bornholm solution is not accurate. As we have said, it has been mathematically proven that the construction of one degree is impossible. However, Bornholm's answer is so close to absolute accuracy that, in practical terms, the deviation plays no part. It amounts to 0.0000015 of a degree. This is about one millionth of a degree from perfection. This is accurate enough to land a spacecraft with precision upon the surface of the moon.

But the builders of Bornholm's churches were not concerned with such matters. They wished to lay out a circle with a circumference of fifty-six English miles. One degree of this circle would measure about 821 feet. If the method which we have just described is employed to construct one degree, then the deviation from absolute perfection would be 0.4 millimetres.

This means that the construction of this one degree on a circle of fifty-six miles would deviate from the exact measure by no more than the diameter of this full stop .

Such sophisticated and advanced knowledge is on a par with the most guarded of state secrets of the modern age. Set against the culture of its time, it is as portentous, and required as much protection, as did the Second World War's development of the atomic bomb.

The spider at the centre of Bornholm's web is a creature so advanced and so apparently alien to its own time, that we need not wonder at the 'awe and reverence' which it may have engendered in its guardians.

Chapter Ten
CONCLUSIONS

This final chapter is headed 'Conclusions'. It is not, however, 'The Conclusion' to this story. Throughout the thirty years of the present research, many books have been written which claim finally to have 'solved' the riddle – to have reached that much searched-for 'Conclusion' to the Rennes-le-Château mystery. To have located Saunière's treasure, or a tomb of Christ, or some other such nonsensical fantasy. This book, however, makes no such claim. It is simply a report of the further strides made along the pathway of discovery. Surprising and illuminating though some of them have been, they serve only to indicate the track to be followed in the search for further understanding.

The first stage of this quest was no more than a treasure hunt. 'What was the source of Bérenger Saunière's wealth?' For many people, that question remains powerfully attractive, even though a treasure of gold and jewels would be ultimately banal, providing nothing more than a simple answer to the simple query. We have already provided what seems to us to be a reasonable explanation for the provenance of the priest's funds.[52] For this money-obsessed age, however, such an undramatic conclusion is not enough. Neither is the unexpected goal to which we have been led.

A treasure house of wealth untold would have been satisfyingly exciting. A treasure house of knowledge will seem, to some people, to be a disappointment.

Most of us find geometry and mathematics stupendously boring. We were glad to leave them behind us when we ended our enforced childhood studies. We are unaware of how vital a part these dull little numbers and proportions play, not merely in upholding our civilisation, but in controlling the very structure of the universe which we inhabit. It is therefore difficult for us to accept that the answer to this extraordinary riddle should be *'no more than'* a geometric layout accomplished hundreds of years in the past. To many of us, this seems an anti-climax – a 'fuss about nothing'. We'd rather have a chest filled with gold and jewels.

Nevertheless, the 'treasure' *has* proved to be a body of knowledge – protected, preserved and passed on, century after century. The puzzle with which we are now confronted seems rather to be: 'Why the secrecy?' At the dawn of the third millennium,

---

[52] See *Key to the Sacred Pattern*, p 130.

this does, indeed, seem to be an enigma which may speak more of our ignorance than of our knowledge. What have we yet to learn – we, who consider ourselves to be so 'advanced' – so 'clever'? What has our civilisation forgotten – or suppressed?

We have grown beyond that stupidity which led to Galileo Galilei being shown the torture instruments in order to persuade him to deny what he knew to be a truth - that the earth revolved around the sun. But we forget how different was the world in which those blind Inquisitors lived. At the very beginning of this book, we stressed the different paradigm to which we must hold, in order to grasp the significance of the discoveries which have been made. We must open our eyes to the world which was – if we are fully to understand the world which is. It is too shallow and facile to assume that what we consider to be unimportant can therefore *have* no importance. Criticism by assumption is evidence of nothing but ignorance.

What more, then, can we learn of this treasure to which we have been led? And why were such pains taken to create and then preserve it? Why did St Bernard of Clairvaux, Archbishop Eskil, Bertrand de Blanchefort and their Templar Order and all those other shadowy initiates who lurk hidden behind them, cherish the knowledge which they possessed and expend so much time, skill, labour and ingenuity in fixing it within the confines of a tiny and remote island? And whence came that knowledge?

To this last question we have no certain answer. But, at least, we have begun to identify some of the gifted players in the subtle and ingenious mediaeval game. For it is undeniable that those who planned and built the churches of Bornholm knew *exactly* what they were doing and why they did it. And centuries were to pass before their skill and knowledge could be matched.

Knowledge … *Baphomet* … *Sophia* … The Wisdom worshipped by the Templars was precious to them and to their mentors. And not only to them. They knew how priceless was the gift which they had inherited and which they had to pass on. They knew that it had to be protected for the generations yet to come. They knew that others must be taught the nature and the use of their bequest.

But the world in which they lived was essentially one of ignorance. The vast majority of human beings were superstitious, illiterate, untaught. The minuscule handful who were capable of understanding and using the treasure, lacked even books in which to disseminate their knowledge. Besides – that knowledge was sacred. It attempted to understand and to define the workings of God's creation and so it was not lightly to be shared. It was guarded, therefore, *solis sacerdotibus* – only for the initiated.

But – why build a pattern of churches? We must attempt an explanation – though this can be no more than our personal and subjective reading of the enigmatic facts of Bornholm and of Rennes-le-Château. Future discoveries will, inevitably, amend or augment the hypothesis, just as our earlier hypotheses have been altered by the detection of the Bornholm layout.

It seems to us that the origin of this body of knowledge will be found to lie in a more distant past than we can yet glimpse. But the shape and the significance of the mathematics and geometry by which it is defined must have been part of a continuing, secret tradition over many generations. At some remote time, the extraordinary coincidence of the Rennes-le-Château Pentacle of Mountains was recognised. Here then, on earth, was the sacred place which resonated with the Music of the Spheres. Here, God-given, was the pattern of Nature.

As the skills developed over the centuries, the expertise required in their understanding and use, became more subtle, more complex, more demanding, more daunting. They were more difficult to teach. Difficult subjects require sophisticated instruction. Where, today, can we learn molecular biology, or sub-atomic physics, if not in an university? And where were the appropriate schools a thousand years and more ago? Not only did the western world lack schools where the master

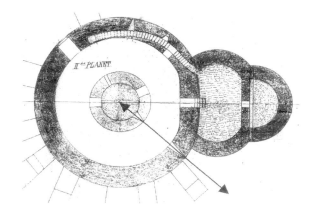

The plan of the upper rotunda of Osterlars church shows the careful alignment of the slit windows to capture the rays of the midwinter solstice sunrise.

mathematicians could teach, it also lacked books. It even lacked the zero – which we find so essential in order simply to add up our mundane supermarket purchases.

And so Bornholm was laid out with absolute precision as a teaching aid. The island proved to be meaningfully placed upon the surface of the earth. In addition, it was small and easily controlled and protected. Above all, it was remote, unknown, unlikely to be disturbed, not big enough or rich enough to attract an errant warrior intent on carving out a kingdom.

Here would the student come to learn, and to learn not merely the mathematics and the geometry. Here also could be taught the underlying symbolism. The mystic and religious undercurrent which would be used in the greater world beyond. It was in that outer world that could be built the mighty gothic cathedrals where God was to be worshipped within a structure built according to His laws. Demonstrating His harmony. Only 'those with the eyes to see and the ears to hear' – only 'the initiated' – would fully understand the wonder that surrounded them.

GUESSING GAME

But, if Bornholm was indeed a place for learning, what was the substance of the wisdom which the teachers wished to impart? How can we begin to approach the fundamentals of the mystery? Perhaps there is more to be uncovered than a mere mathematical treatise.

Having glimpsed at least some of the participants in this fascinating game, is it possible to guess at the cards which were held in the players' hands? We can, of course, do no more than guess. Even so, the attempt to understand can provide tantalising hints of a possible underlying truth. A guess cannot become a certainty while secrets yet remain, though the game may be fruitful – as well as entertaining.

The Square and the Circle. Nylars square tower stands out against its round church. Nylars is dedicated to St Nicholas (Nilaus or Nils).

The strongest suit in our hand is, of course, the geometry. But we also have Bérenger Saunière, the poor nineteenth century French priest who became rich. We have nine mediaeval French knights who spent nine years burrowing beneath Jerusalem and who returned to Europe as the Knights Templar, to become one of the strongest and wealthiest organisations of their day. We have Bertrand de Blanchefort, their Grand Master, elected in the last year of the life of their protector, the Burgundian nobleman St Bernard of Clairvaux. Then there is Bernard's friend, the Danish archbishop Eskil. There is Bornholm. And, of course, there is Rennes-le-Château.

There are other cards, which are only partly visible. The Burgundian nobility, with origins on Bornholm, were descendants also of a dynasty of French kings, the Merovingians, and claimed to be, like Jesus, of the house and lineage of David. In this suit are other cards: Mount Sion in Jerusalem, where the Templars dug in the twelfth century, and where, in 1909, the Swedish engineer, Johan Millén, led his English Parker Expedition on their clandestine subterranean hunt for the Ark of the Covenant, led by the Old Testament cipher unravelled by the Finn, Dr Juvelius.

Can these diverse cards be shuffled in a meaningful way? Can we construct a hand that shows the chance of winning a glimpse of the real underlying story? We must attempt to match the suits. We must ask the simple questions.

First: if the nine original knights of the Templar Order were, indeed, really looking for something in Jerusalem … how did they know where to look? Clearly, they must have known what they were doing. Second: whence came the knowledge? What was the background against which their search was set?

It was in their recent past that Jerusalem had been wrested from Islam by the united force of the Christian crusading armies. Godefroi de Bouillon had been offered, and had refused, the crown. Instead he chose to be 'Protector of the Holy Sepulchre'. When he died, shortly after, it was his brother Baudouin who assumed the resonant title of 'King of Jerusalem'. If the brothers were, as it seems, descended from the Merovingian kings and were thus of the House of David, their assumption of authority could well have been a well-prepared plan for the reinstatement of the rightful royal house.[53]

Godefroi and Baudouin were of the nobility of Lower Lorraine, the dukedom adjacent to Burgundy and, of course, Clairvaux. Again we are confronting the small and enclosed world of the aristocratic group who stood behind the foundation of both Cistercians and Templars. Now there is a wild card to play. King Charles XIII and his curious Swedish Freemasonry, which holds the 'secret' documents of Starck. The hidden, inner order of masonic 'Templars', who adopted the Essene custom of calling their master 'the Father of Wisdom'.

These cards can, indeed, be shuffled into an interesting hand. Bernard of Clairvaux can be set beside the Finnish Dr Juvelius, to offer an assumption. Did Bernard, like Juvelius so many centuries later, know of the Old Testament code? Hugh Schonfield demonstrated that the Templars were certainly aware of such a

---

[53] See *The Holy Blood and the Holy Grail*.

cipher. Such secrets seem to have been accessible. And here is a straightforward line of connection. Old Testament … Essenes … Davidic descent … Merovingians … Burgundians … Bernard … Knights Templar. The thread may appear tenuous – but it is there.

St Bernard is a key figure, the *éminence grise* with some additional and unexpected cards to play. When the tomb of the fifth-century Merovingian king, Childeric, was opened, three hundred golden bees were found among the grave's contents. The Emperor Napoleon chose to have these sewn onto his coronation robe. What significance lies in these tiny images of gold?

In our game the bee can make an evocative contribution. The industrious creature fashions cells of a remarkably accurate and meaningful geometric form – the hexagon., the equilateral six-sided figure which forms the Star of David. And St Bernard chose as his seal, the beehive.

Now let us extend our game of assumptions into an even more uncertain area, but still one that conforms to the cards which we have found in our hand.

Let us suppose that Bernard possessed the same cipher, which later was to lead Millén to uncover a secret labyrinth deep within Mount Ophel. Millén was convinced that the Ark of the Covenant was his ultimate goal. What would such a quest have meant to Bernard and to his family? Here would have been a veritable treasure beyond price, the rightful inheritance of the descendants of David's line.

The next move in the game would then have been an extremely secret operation whose objective would be the recovery and securing of the sacred objects. The task to be entrusted to the nine knights who were to become the founding group of the Poor Soldiers of Christ and the Temple of Solomon, among whom was Bernard's uncle, his mother's brother, André de Montbard.

The Templars take their vows in the Church of the Holy Sepulchre and declare their objective – to protect the pilgrim roads to Jerusalem. But there is no evidence that they engaged in any such activity. Can the new 'Millén' card in our hand suggest an alternative game plan?

If the real and covert purpose was the retrieval of sacred objects, these would obviously have enormous religious import. Swedish Freemasonry purports to be a secret offshoot of the Templar Order, based on the belief that Christianity is a continuation of the true and original Judaic faith preserved and practised by the 'Sons of Zadoch' and established in the Essene society at Qumran, prior to the birth of Jesus. The shuffling of the cards produce further fascinating possibilities.

If this is the correct play, then perhaps 'the protection of the pilgrim roads to Jerusalem' is not a false statement. It could now appear to be rather more akin to an allegory – a symbolic statement of a true purpose. The pilgrim roads lead not to an earthly, but to a heavenly Jerusalem. The ultimate goal of the Christian – to live his life in accord with the law of God; the Commandments preserved and kept secure within the Ark.

In the light of our glimpses of a hidden scientific knowledge, perhaps the Ark of the Covenant contains something else? Something which could affect our understanding of Christianity? A combination of religion and of a science which would have been viewed as heresy in the Middle Ages? This would have been a card which the Templars would have had to keep well hidden. The protection of the pilgrim roads, becomes the protection of a hidden truth and its preservation for the benefit of humankind. What, one must ask, could the Templars have discovered as they cleared the Stables of Solomon?

Of course, it is only possible to speculate. But the shadow of the mystery bears a faintly familiar outline. Unquestionably, the return of the Templars saw the flowering of a hitherto unknown scientific knowledge which is demonstrated in the building of the gothic cathedrals as well as in the Bornholm layout. Could it be that this visible inheritance is no more than a part of the wisdom which was acquired and which reaches back into the mists of time. Could Solomon's Temple have contained far, far more treasure than we can yet imagine?

In this hypothetical version of the game, the truth buried in the heart of Mount Sion would have been of inestimable value. The Grail sought by the knight who 'Pierced the Vale'. Here would have lain the object of the quest, the finding of which, the Templars told St Bernard, they had accomplished.

The next cards fall simply. In 1127, nine years after their foundation, the nine Templars return to Europe. Bernard of Clairvaux assures the pope's approval of the new Order and a few years later they are granted their autonomous status. They are exempt from allegiance to any king or prelate. Henceforth, they are answerable only to the pope. Wealth, possessions and power flow in, as well as respect and admiration from the royal houses of Europe. This postulated game could explain many of the mysteries which encompass the Order.

But our hand is not yet exhausted. When the Danish archbishop Eskil visited Clairvaux in 1162, for the preparation of the Baltic Mission, our game would suggest that the planning was made in close concert with both Templars and Cistercians. This is made clear by the following facts:

1. It was a Cistercian monk who was appointed bishop of pagan Estonia in 1164, answering directly to Eskil.
2. The Cistercian monastery of Roma was founded in the same year, 1164, on the Baltic island of Gothland, which was the nearest Christian shore to Estonia.
3. In little more than a decade, monks from Danish Cistercian monasteries had founded four new establishments at the southern (pagan) end of the Baltic Sea.
4. It was Theoderic, a Cistercian monk, who established a division of the Templars at Riga in 1202.

This hand clearly shows how deep was the involvement of Cistercians and Templars, as well as Eskil, in the Baltic planning from at least as early as 1164. And the Templars' presiding master at this time was Bertrand de Blanchefort, who must, inevitably, have played a leading role in the decision-making. The Rennes-le-Château card has reappeared.

Bertrand, it should be remembered, was elected Grand Master in the last months of St Bernard's life. It is too easy for us merely to see such events within a chronological framework, without considering their interaction. Bernard was coming to the end of his days. Like any leader, the future of the organisations over which he presided, must have occupied his thoughts. The choice of Bertrand de Blanchefort to lead his Templars into an uncertain future could not have been made upon a whim. Even if the eventual downfall of the Order was not envisaged, the autonomy of the Templars might have seemed less unassailable once St Bernard's protection was no longer assured. It is not too wild a guess to assume that Bertrand de Blanchefort may have had certain qualities, talents or experience, which Bernard considered to be valuable.

If the Templars' accomplished task had indeed been the rescue of lost and sacred objects, then the need for a secure hiding place would have been paramount. And Bertrand de Blanchefort's part in the Rennes-le-Château story has already linked him with enigmatic tales of treasure. In 1156, we are told, three years after his election as Grand Master, Bertrand brought German-speaking miners to the Languedoc, where they supposedly exploited the ancient Roman gold and silver workings.

These 'miners', unable to communicate with the local populace, were further segregated by the establishment of a special court – *la Judicature des Allemands* – to deal with any complications which might arise during their stay. In the seventeenth century, one César d'Arcons, with a team of engineers, examined the mineralogical possibilities of the area. In his report, d'Arcons deals with the evidence of the activity left by Bertrand de Blanchefort's twelfth century German workers. They do not appear, he concludes, to have been engaged in mining. He suggests that they may, perhaps, have been melting down metal objects – or constructing some kind of crypt or hiding place.[54] And our game suggests that Bertrand's Templars may have had something to hide. The play grows more coherent.

Why choose Rennes-le-Château? Our hand of cards could play yet one more tempting trick. The village saint is Mary of Magdala. Legend tells us that she came to France, bringing with her the Holy Grail. More precious things from Jerusalem – precious to the Jewish Princedom established here so long before. If here indeed lay hidden treasure, protected and preserved through generations and concealed within a place whose natural geometry was 'God-given', then this may well be the

[54] César d'Arcons, *Du Flux et reflux de la mer ...*, Paris 1667.

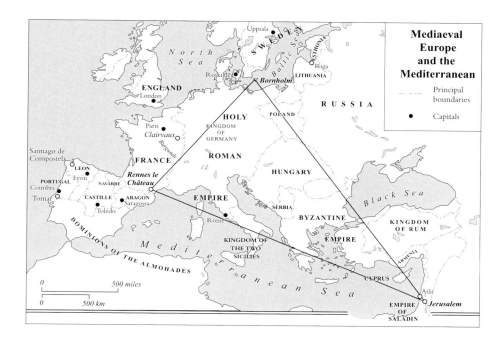

special gift which Bertrand de Blanchefort could bring to the enterprise. Knowledge of a geometric system which for centuries had been 'laid out' and marked by sacred structures, forming a landscape which both protected and indicated a sure hiding place.

With St Bernard's death, the Templars had lost a bulwark. It would make sense to forearm against future possible vulnerability. It would make sense to conceal whatever may have been the Order's treasures in more than one place. Better still to provide a hiding place which was remote and had no apparent connection with the Order. Bertrand's involvement in the planning for the Baltic Mission would have offered him the perfect precautionary opportunity. Bornholm, of no previous importance, now becomes a trump card.

The tricks in our game of cards begin to mount. This hypothetical run of play is capable of explaining many of the stranger elements in the mystery. It explains why there is geometry on Bornholm. More ... it explains why the geometry is so firmly linked to Rennes-le-Château. And there is another and hitherto unseen card which we can now add to our hand. Excavations were undertaken in 1955, in connection with the laying of heating ducts beneath the floor of Østerlars church. The official report of the archaeologist who supervised the work describes unusual and unexpected stone features below the church floor, which might be explained by the presence of an undiscovered crypt. Olsker church also has the curious indication of

The curious blocked entry beneath Olsker's staircase.

a possible underground structure beneath a staircase. Neither of these subterranean anomalies has, thus far, been investigated.

But we are playing a game. And the game has more than one player. Have we been dealt an honest hand? Or are some of the cards marked? Are we playing the game according to an opponent's set of rules?

The Saunière story began to filter out in the 1960s. Thirty years of research have taught us that many of the original givens of the story are unreliable - even false. We can no longer even be certain that Saunière found a treasure. The famous hollow altar pillar has proved to be less hollow, and more equivocal, than we were led to believe. Why did the questionable *Prieuré de Sion* attract our attention and disseminate so many intriguing possibilities – none of which had anything (apparently) to do with the unquestionable geometry to which we have been led?

The game remains a game – even though it is clear that, down the centuries, the play has sometimes held great hazard and sometimes more subtle ingenuity. Our investigations have shown that the Earth was indeed measured with great accuracy in a very remote past, and that amazing fact is preserved in the English measure system. Other antique measures have disappeared. The Egyptian cubit, the Hebrew sacred cubit, the gizabethe – all are forgotten.

It is strange that, even now, as this book is being written, the English measure is under threat and attempts are being made to consign it, too, to oblivion. One must wonder why the English mile was fixed by Statute, as an irrelevance in a sixteenth century Act of Parliament, which has nothing to do with measure? Why was it done at a time when Parliament was not even in session? Who was the anonymous figure with the power to make the decision and enact the law?

Our game would have us suggest that there are shadowy figures hovering at the edge of our vision and who are ensuring, as the centuries pass, that the precious knowledge is not lost. Has the *Prieuré de Sion*, or some organisation like it, been protecting secret knowledge, if not secret artefacts, down the centuries? Was the *Prieuré*, or some organisation like it, by filtering strange and intriguing stories out into the greater world, attempting to attract brethren with whom it had lost touch over the years and who would recognise the curious symbols emblazoned on the playing cards?

As with our hypothetical card game, it is possible to invent, to imagine, to embroider upon, the few fragile threads of the story. Only the Bornholm layout remains solid, firm, substantial. On Bornholm was created, preserved and handed on the true 'Treasure Beyond Price'. No hoard of gold or jewels was ever more precious.

We are the heirs to genius. Should we not be satisfied? Should we not cease to ask the questions? Should we not cease to wonder? Should we not turn to our inheritance and try to learn from it?

POSTSCRIPT

Since this book was first published in November 2000, some astonishing further discoveries have been made. Following our suggestion (pp 137/8) that underground anomalies in the Bornholm churches might be worth investigating, a geo-radar survey has identified what seems to be a hitherto unknown crypt beneath Østerlars Church. Coincidentally, a similar survey has also been undertaken at Rennes-le-Château. This, too, has produced evidence of a crypt beneath the church as well as another anomaly, (possibly a chest or coffer), buried under Saunière's *Tour Magdala*.

Such discoveries can, of course, easily be sensationalised and lead to familiar speculations concerning the possibility of buried treasure and/or biblical revelations. Permission to investigate further has been requested of the appropriate authorities. Not surprisingly, the mills of officialdom – quite properly – grind exceedingly slow. We await the eventual outcome with interest. However, it should be said that, while a golden hoard might generate excitement, it would be unlikely to help any understanding of the geometric enigma which we have been exploring. And along this path, too, further strides have been made.

Much more interesting and important than a buried treasure has been the revelation of a basic structural fact concerning the Bornholm design itself. As with all such valid and significant discoveries, it is of an obvious simplicity. So obvious that, despite our careful examination and re-examination of all the details when we were first preparing for publication, we had not noticed what was staring us in the face. It was the answer to a simple question: could there be a significance in the apparently arbitrary bearing of the prime axis of the design (Østerlars/Nylars)? We can now demonstrate that the chosen azimuth of this line proves that the entire Bornholm system is carefully – and with extreme accuracy – oriented towards True North.

If a right angled triangle is constructed as in the figure (right), so that one side has a length of 1 and the hypotenuse has length √7 ÷ √3 – then the smallest angle in this triangle will be 40.89...°. The presence of √7 ÷ √3 in diagrams 8 & 9 (pp 162-3) shows that the system is unquestionably oriented to achieve this.

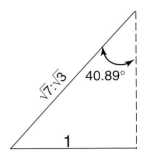

We must point out, however, that when the azimuth of the axis is calculated from the official co-ordinates, the angle proves to be 40.78...° from True North. The hypothesised theoretical angle thus _seems_ to show a discrepency of (40.89 – 40.78 =) 0.11°. While this is extraordinarily close, the system is, in fact, much more accurate than this.

When using the co-ordinate system, the calculated azimuth of a particular line is not always the angle of that line to True North. This is because all north/south lines in the co-ordinate system are parallel. In reality, of course, the lines are _not parallel_, since they are directed toward the same point: i.e. the North Pole. There will thus be a discrepency between the direction of a line towards north, <u>when calculated from the co-ordinates,</u> (referred to as Net North) – and the same line's direction towards True North <u>as viewed from a specific geographical point</u>.

At our request, the _Kort & Matrikelstyrelsen_ has calculated the azimuth of the Østerlars/Nylars/Christianø axis, when measured respectively from Nylars, Østerlars and the Christiansø Compass Point.

As can be seen in the diagram (below), the azimuth of this line, when measured from Østerlars (the centre of the system), is 40.86...°, compared with the theoretical angle of 40.89...°.

The discrepancy is (40.89... – 40.86...° =) 0.03 degrees.

Even without the reminder that the Bornholm churches were built almost a thousand years ago, this is astonishingly precise. Perhaps the secrets – if any – which await within the newly discovered hiding places may help us to understand and appreciate yet more the amazing skills of our ancestors?

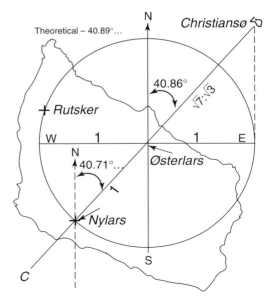

Part Four
CALCULATIONS

Solis Sacerdotibus

Only for the Initiated

Chapter Eleven
THE GEOMETRICAL KEY

The authors wish to express their grateful thanks to Niels Lind, Distinguished Professor Emeritus at the University of Waterloo, Victoria, BC, Canada, for the painstaking care with which he has checked and verified the calculations in this Chapter (See his letter over). Also to James R. Smith for his guidance with the proper presentation of the material.

The location in the landscape of the four round churches of Bornholm: Østerlars, Nylars, Olsker and Nyker, indicates an unusual but very beautiful geometrical pattern. In addition, the round churches reveal the key to further landscape geometry, which is linked to the other medieval churches on the island. In the following pages, we shall analyse this geometrical key, in order that we may be able to demonstrate its unusual elegance, as well as the role which it plays in the calculation of the geometrical system. To make this analysis we must begin by defining and then constructing the geometry indicated by the four round churches.

N.B. The following pages may prove difficult for the non-mathematically educated reader who, rather than struggle with the unaccustomed calculations, may, perhaps, rather wish to take them on trust. The conclusions – as well as other readily assimilated pieces of evidence – will be found indicated by text-boxes and/or in bold type.

NOTE : Three churches have been omitted from this investigation. They are Pedersker, Aakirke, and Østermarie. Pedersker is the only one of Bornholm's churches which is generally agreed to have been built upon a much older, pre-existing wooden structure. The site was therefore chosen at an earlier date and would not have been part of the layout design.

Aakirke and Østermarie however have, for the present, been omitted, although their place in the over-all conception can be demonstrated. Their function appears to be different from that of the twelve forming the demonstrated geometric design. Their separate and more complex intent, recently identified, makes them difficult to fit into the present study – which is already sufficiently complex. It can, however, be pointed out that they are separated by exactly six English miles and their alignment provides a direct connection with Rennes-le-Château.

Niels C. Lind

Distinguished Professor Emeritus, University of Waterloo, FRSC, FAAM, M. Sc., Ph. D.

Monday, March 22, 1999

Erling Haagensen

Subject: Location of Medieval Churches on Bornholm

Here are the results of (1) my review of your calculations of the theoretical coordinates of several churches on Bornholm and (2) my comparison with the measured coordinates in System 45. Also, (3) some comments on your question (I paraphrase) whether the coincidence between theoretical and observed coordinates, such as it is, could be due to chance. Finally, I provide (4) some comments on the accuracy with which a survey to position the churches according to a scheme such as the one you suggest, could have been carried out in the terrain of Bornholm in the Middle Ages by medieval techniques and equipment.

(1) I calculated the coordinates of 12 churches and four auxiliary points according to the layout you specify in your Appendix, using a double precision computer spreadsheet. *I have not discovered any errors in your calculations.*

(2) Disregarding the five unverifiable points (four auxiliary points and Poulsker), I calculated the coordinates of the centroid of the remaining 11 churches in your layout *("the map")* and in the terrain according to System 45. I made no correction for displacements from observed points to altars. I then translated the map to the centroid in the terrain, rotated the map 40.766 deg. and determined the map scale (1: 14,344.55)in order to minimize the sum of the squares of the discrepancy between the 11 points (RMS error 24.8 m). Maximum error is 42.2 m (Olsker). *These values essentially confirm your analysis.*

(3) Could the near coincidence between the theoretical and observed coordinates be due to chance? I do not know how to answer this question, because it is not the nature of your theory to make several "blind" predictions of the location of objects that *subsequently* could be observed.

(4) It is interesting to consider how medieval surveyors could have laid out a design such as "the map" in the field and positioned the churches. I have several years experience with similar field work, albeit using mid-20th century technology. I have no knowledge of what instruments and procedures they can have used, but they probably laid out open traverses in the terrain, sighting by eye and chaining distances with metal chains without correcting for temperature, sag and slope. I believe they could not achieve accuracies better than 1:2000 in the measured lengths over 10-20 km distances in fairly wooded and hilly terrain and 0.01 degree in directions. This would give RMS errors of at least 7 m, roughly. *An RMS error of about 24.8 m, as found in (2) above is not incompatible with the belief that the churches were located according to a plan such as "the map."*

Sincerely

Niels Lind

DEFINITION OF THE KEY

In the pages which follow, our intention is to demonstrate the accuracy of the layout of the twelve mediaeval churches, by a comparison of their actual positions with the calculated theoretical points. To achieve this, the theoretical geometry must be precisely defined. Since it has become evident that the Bornholm System demonstrates hitherto unknown geometrical approximations, it has been necessary to define the theoretical co-ordinates more precisely than would be normal in land surveying practise.

The first stage is a description of the manner in which the layout of the four round churches is controlled by the theoretical 'Geometric Key'. The next stage demonstrates how the Key also controls the placing of the remaining eight churches.

For a comparison of the actual with the theoretical position of each church, the actual positions of the round churches of Østerlars and Nylars are used to define the size and orientation of the theoretical geometry. Their actual positions are then used to define a new co-ordinate system, within which the theoretical points are calculated.

The analysis is performed in three stages: 1. Definition of the geometry. 2. Calculation of the positions of the theoretical points. 3. Calculation of the deviation of the actual from the theoretical position of each church.

Østerlars:

With a point 1 as centre, we draw a circle of unit radius 1.

> **Point 1 is the theoretical position of Østerlars church.**

Nylars :

A random diameter is drawn - and the centre of the circle **(Point 1)** is chosen as the centre of a co-ordinate system. This diameter is the **Y - axis** of the system.

The negative Y-axis intersects the circle at **Point 2.**

> **Point 2 is the theoretical position of Nylars church.**

Diagram 1

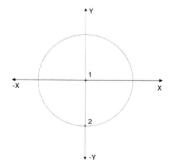

Olsker:

The circumscribed square is constructed around the circle such that the sides are parallel to the axes.

Diagram 2

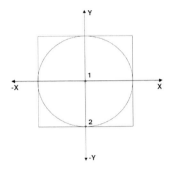

The circumscribed circle is constructed around this square.
(The radius of this circle = √2.)
This circle intersects the co-ordinate system's positive Y-axis in Point 106 - and the negative Y-axis in Point 121.

Diagram 3

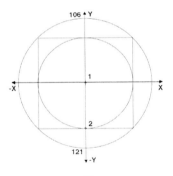

Diagram 4

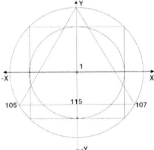

In the circle r = √2 we construct an inscribed equilateral triangle oriented such that one vertex is at Point 106. The triangle's other vertices are called 105 (with negative X-value) - and 107 (with positive X-value). Each side in this triangle has length = ($\sqrt{2}$ x $\sqrt{3}$) = $\sqrt{6}$. The line from 105 to 107 intersects the Y-axis at Point 115.

The next step of the geometry is to construct an equilateral triangle so defined, that its centre is placed in Point 2 - and one of its sides is placed on line 105-107.

Diagram 5

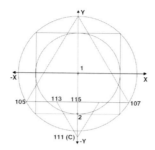

Line segment 2 to 115 is marked out twice on the Y-axis from Point 2 in the direction away from 1. The Point thus found is called 111.

(Note: Point 111 is referred to in Chapter Four and Five and in some of the following calculations as the Point C.)

111 to 115 will be normal (i.e. at 90°) to line 105 to 107 and from the construction of 111, line 111 to 115 is an altitude in the acquired triangle.

From the Point 111 we construct a 30 degree angle with one leg being line 111 to 115 - and the other leg being constructed to the left in the co-ordinate system. This leg intersects line 105 to 115 at Point 113. The line 111 to 113 is thus a side in the required equilateral triangle.

Diagram 5a

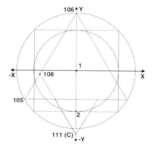

The side 111 to 113 is now extended on the other side of 113 until the line intersects line 105 to 106. This intersection is called 108.

Point 108 is the theoretical position of Olsker church.

The seemingly randomly placed Point 108 is a much more interesting geometric location than it appears. This becomes evident when the hexagon is included in the design.

Diagram 5b

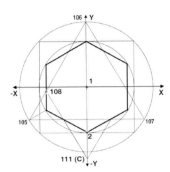

It is now possible to appreciate the extraordinary interplay of the geometric figures. Point 108 lies on the face of the large equilateral triangle (105-106-107). It is positioned exactly where the hexagon cuts that face. And it does more than this. The line 108 to 111 also creates two small equilateral triangles whose centres are defined by two of the points of the six-sided shape. There is an undeniable elegance in the way that the faces of the hexagon merge with the bisections of the angles of the small triangles.

Later elements of this investigation will uncover even more layers of significance in the placing of this controlling Point 108.

Diagram 5c

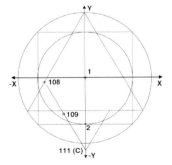

Nyker:

From Point 108 in the direction of Point 111 is marked out the distance of $\sqrt{7} : \sqrt{3} : 2$. The thus acquired Point is called 109.

> **Point 109 is the theoretical position of Nyker church.**

Note: It is important to stress, that the distance √7 : √3 : 2 has importance within the geometry. It is the length of the radius in the inscribed circle of an equilateral triangle with sides √7. Such a triangle seems to have a specific relationship to ancient systems of measurement. This relationship is explained in chapter 5.

There are several possible constructions for the distance √7 : √3 : 2.

One is as follows:

Construct a right triangle with sides √2 and √5.

(√2 is the length of the diagonal in a square with the side 1; √5 is the length of the diagonal in a rectangle with the sides 1 and 2).

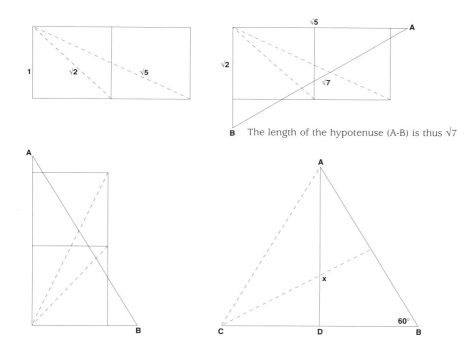

The length of the hypotenuse (A-B) is thus √7

An angle of 60 degrees is constructed. One leg (A - B) is marked out with length √7. This line is then divided into two equal segments. The other leg is marked out with length √7 : 2, (B - D). By connecting points A - D, a triangle (A - B - D) is formed. Due to the 60 degree angle and the ratio between the sides being 1 and 2, this triangle is right-angled.

The hypotenuse (A-B) is thus the side of an equilateral triangle (A-B-C) with sides √7. The perpendicular (D-A) is intersected by the line connecting C to the mid-point of A - B. The intersection point (x) splits the perpendicular (D-A) into two segments. The smaller of these (x-D) has length √7 : √3 : 2.

ANALYSIS OF THE 'KEY'

The Key

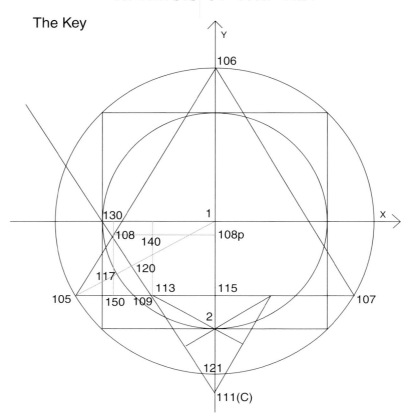

We shall begin by proving, that Point 108 (Olsker) is also placed on a side of the hexagon, inscribed in the original circle r = 1, and is orientated such that two of its vertices lie on the Y-axis.

We introduce the following additional points:

The equilateral triangle 105, 108, 113 has as centre Point 117 - and the altitude from 105 intersects side 108 to 113 in Point 120 (see diagram above).

2 to 115 = (1 to 2) - (1 to 115) = 1 - 1: 2 x √2

111 to 115 = 3 x (2 to 115) = 3 - 3 : 2 x √2

113 to 115 = 1: √3 x (111 to 115) = 1: √3 x (3 - 3:2 x √2) = 3 : √3 - 3 : √3 x 2 x √2

105 to 113 = (105 to 115) - (113 to 115) = 1 : 2 x √2 x √3 - 3 : √3 + 3 : √3 x 2 x √2

105 to 120 = 1 : 2 x √3 x (105 to 113) = 3 : 2 x √2 - 3 : 2

117 to 120 = (radius of circle inscribed in triangle 105-108-113) = 1 : 3 x (105 to 120) = 1 : 2 x √2 -1 : 2

117 to 108 = (radius of circle circumscribed to triangle 105 - 108 - 113) = 2 x (117 to 120) = $\sqrt{2}$ - 1

Point 117 is at the centre of triangle 105-108-113.

Since the altitude 105 to 120 in this triangle bisects angle 105, line 105 to 120 must be a part of line 1 to 105, which is a radius in the circle circumscribing triangle 105 - 106 - 107.

117 must thus be on this line.

105 to 117 = 108 to 117 = $\sqrt{2}$ - 1

1 to 105 = (radius in the circumscribing circle) = $\sqrt{2}$

1 to 117 = (1 to 105) - (105 to 117) = 1

From this it follows that 117 lies on the original circle (r = 1).
The angle between 1 to 106 and 1 to 105 is 120 degrees - thus, angle 2 - 1 - 105 must be 60 degrees.
From this it follows, that line 2 - 117 equals the side of a regular hexagon inscribed in the original circle (r = 1).
Thus line segment 2 to 117 is of unit length.

The altitude from 108 in triangle 105 - 108 - 113 is normal to line 105 to 115; thus 117 to 108 is parallel to 1 to 2 - and, since distance 117 to 108 is less than unity, it follows that Point 108 lies on a side of a regular hexagon, inscribed in the original circle - with one vertex in Point 2 and the neighbouring vertex in Point 117. **QED.**

At the same time it is demonstrated, that **the Point 108 intersects the side of the hexagon in the proportion** 1 : ([$\sqrt{2}$ - 1] : [2 - $\sqrt{2}$]) = 1 : $\sqrt{2}$.

From this we may say, that Point 108 (Olsker) indicates some unusual but very "beautiful" geometric relations.

CALCULATIONS - CO-ORDINATES

From the above geometrical analysis, it is possible to calculate the co-ordinates of the four points, indicated by the positions of the round churches.
Further calculations give :

1 to 111 = (111 to 115) + (1 to 115) = (3 - 3:2 x $\sqrt{2}$) + 1:2 x $\sqrt{2}$ = 3 - $\sqrt{2}$

121 to 111 = (1 to 111) - (1 to 121) = 3 - $\sqrt{2}$ - $\sqrt{2}$ = 3 - 2 x $\sqrt{2}$

Let Point 108p be the projection of Point 108 on the Y-axis. Then:

1 to 108p = 1:2 - (117 to 108) = 1:2 - ($\sqrt{2}$ - 1) = 3:2 - $\sqrt{2}$ (= 1:2 x [111 to 121])

From this we can calculate the co-ordinates of Point 108:

Y:

The corresponding numerical value of the Y-co-ordinate to 108 is equal to the distance

(1-108p) = **3:2 - √2 = 0.085786438**

X:

The altitude from 108 is constructed in triangle 105-108-113.

It intersects the side 105 to 113 in Point 150.

This altitude is extended on the other side of 108 to intersect the X-axis in the Point 130.

The X-axis is parallel to the side 105 to 113.

From this it follows that 108 to 117 is normal to the X-axis.

117-130-1 is thus a right triangle.

This triangle's angle 1 is 30 degrees.

Thus the distance 1 to 130 (the numerical value of the X-co-ordinate to Point 108 (Olsker)) = √3 : 2 x (1-117) = **√3 : 2 = 0.866025404**

From this we can calculate the co-ordinates of Point 109 (Nyker)

Y:

From triangle 108-109-140 the side 109 to 140 equals √3 x (140 to 108) = √7 : 4.

The y-co-ordinate to 109 is thus the numerical value of the distance 109 to 109p:

(109 to 140) + (140 to 109p) = **√7:4 + 3 : 2 - √2 = 0.747224265**

X:

The projection of 109 on the Y-axis is called 109p.

The line 109 to 109p intersects 108 to 108p in Point 140.

From this it follows that triangle 108-140-109 is a right triangle with angle 109 equal to 30 degrees.

Thus, the length of side 108 to 140 equals (108 to 109 : 2) = √7: √3:4.

The numerical value of the X-co-ordinate of Point 109 is thus:

108p to 140 = 108 to 108p - 108 to 140 = **√3 : 2 - √7 : √3 : 4 = 0.484144096.**

From the above calculation it is possible to list the co-ordinates of the theoretical points of the four round churches:

Østerlars (Point 1):	Nylars (Point 2):	Olsker (Point 108)	Nyker (Point 109):
Y = 0	Y = -1	Y = 0.085786438	Y = 0.747224265
X = 0	X = 0	X = 0.866025404	X = 0.484144096

CALCULATIONS OF THEORETICAL CO-ORDINATES WITHIN 'SYSTEM 45 BORNHOLM'

The official survey of the Island of Bornholm was carried out by the Danish Government mapping office known as the *Kort & Matrikelstyrelsen* and is designated System 45 Bornholm. The co-ordinates of the towers of all the mediaeval churches on the island were calculated for the survey and can be found in the table on page 177. *Kort & Matrikelstyrelsen* confirms that System 45 is defined from a point in the antenna of a tower known as *"Kongemindet"* which is situated in the centre of the island. This point is given the co-ordinates :

$$X = 50\ 000.00\ Y = 50\ 000.00$$

This means, that the system is based solely upon measures on the island - and, since the system covers an area of 50 by 50 kilometres (maximum), the deviation in co- ordinates from the present plane projection to the corresponding spherical geometry calculations, has no practical influence.

The system's X-axis is oriented from East towards West (the X-co-ordinate increases in the westerly direction).

The system's Y-axis is oriented from South towards North (the Y-co-ordinate increases in the northerly direction) - which is normal.

This means that the system is left-handed.

In the following, will be found calculations of the co-ordinates of all the theoretical, geometrical points, described in the Chapters Four and Five - within the System 45 Bornholm.
After each calculation, the co-ordinates of the theoretical points are compared with the measured co-ordinates in the table on page 177.
It is thus possible to establish the exact position of any theoretical point in relation to the tower of the corresponding church. By means of the architectural ground plans of the churches (when they are available) - it is possible to demonstrate exactly where the theoretical point is located in relation to the position of the mediaeval church - as shown in the illustrations in the Chapters Four and Five.

1: Østerlars.

The church of Østerlars defines the centre of the geometry. The existing co-ordinates are calculated to the tip of the concentric church roof - and thus correspond to a point in the centre of the round church.

The following comparison between the actual and theoretical co-ordinates is, in general, made with reference to the most significant place in the church, i.e. the altar.

Since the altar in Østerlars is placed 10.6 m due East of the centre of the church (from the ground plan of the church found in the archives of the Danish National Museum), the theoretical centre of the system is found by subtracting 10.6 metres from the X co-ordinate of Østerlars.

Actual co-ordinates (see table at page 177) to the church spire (the centre of the round church):

$$Y = 56\ 658.79 \qquad X = 45\ 385.33$$

Theoretical co-ordinates of the centre of the geometry (The altar of Østerlars - 10.6 metres due east of the church centre)

Østerlars:
$Y = 56\ 658.79$
$X = 45\ 385.33 - 10.6 = 45\ 374.73$

2: **Nylars**

The Østerlars-Nylars line defines the size and the orientation of the geometry.
We are using the altars of Østerlars and Nylars as reference - but, for practical reasons, we have calculated the geometry in round figures.

The distance Østerlars-Nylars is consequently **defined by us** as exactly 14 336 metres, and the orientation of the line from Østerlars to Nylars (the orientation of the Y-axis in our local geometry) is defined as having an azimuth of exactly 40.78°. These rounded figures are in accordance with the length and orientation of a line between the altars of Nylars and Østerlars - as shown in a later calculation.

By use of a Texas Instruments GALAXY 40x it is possible directly to calculate polar and Cartesian co-ordinates.

Using the polar co-ordinates:

$$Y = -(90° - 40.78°) = -49.22° \quad X = 14\ 336$$

we find the Cartesian co-ordinates

$$Y = -10\ 855.55031 \qquad\qquad X = 9\ 363.649047$$

Adding these co-ordinates to the theoretical co-ordinates of Østerlars, we find **the theoretical co-ordinates of**

Nylars:
$Y = 56\ 658.79 - 10\ 855.55031 = 45\ 803.23969$
$X = 45\ 374.73 + 9\ 363.649047 = 54\ 738.37905$

Note:

Since the co-ordinates are defined by us (for practical reasons) to be rounded figures, we compare with the actual Nylars co-ordinates of the church spire (the centre of the church):

Y = 45 803,09

X = 54 748.17

The Y co-ordinate, defined by us, is thus:

45 803.09 - 45 803.24 = 0.15 metres South of the actual co-ordinate.

The X co-ordinate, defined by us, is:

54 738.38 - 54 748.17 = 9.79 metres East of the actual co-ordinate.

> **This position, relative to the centre of the church, (as verified from the ground plan found in the archives of the Danish National Museum), coincides with the position of the altar of Nylars Church.**

The use of the (round) distance 14 336 metres and the (round) azimuth 40.78° is thus justified, because it means that the **exact position of the altars in the churches of Østerlars and Nylars define the geometrical key as described above. The positions of these altars consequently define the following geometry.**

The names of the churches in the following section refer to **the corresponding theoretical geometrical points,** as defined through the description of the "geometrical key" above and in the description of the geometry in Chapters Four and Five.

From the above, it is possible to calculate the theoretical co-ordinates of each point as follows:

3: Olsker

The co-ordinates of Olsker, (Point 108), within the System 45 Bornholm, can be found from the calculations above by transferring the theoretical co-ordinates to the actual co-ordinates of system 45 Bornholm.

Olsker (108) from the above:

$Y = -(3{:}2 - \sqrt{2}) = -0.085786438$

$X = -\sqrt{3}{:}2 = -0.866025404$

By use of a calculator, we find the corresponding polar co-ordinates:

Angle = - 174.342870152°

Distance = 0.870263933

Our theoretical 1 is identical to: **14 336** metres within System 45 Bornholm.

The inclination of the axis in our theoretical system is **40.78°**, measured clockwise from the axis of System 45 Bornholm.

NOTE:

We must remember that the co-ordinate-system 45 Bornholm is laterally reversed in the Y-axis. Thus, in System 45 Bornholm, an azimuth of 40.78 degrees is calculated clockwise, (from the X-axis (West) over the Y-axis (North)), as (90° + 40.78° =) 130.78°. Or anti-clockwise (from the X-axis (West) over the Y-axis (South) over the X-axis (East)) as (- 90° - 90° - [90° - 40.78°]) = - 229.22°.

Thus we are able to transfer the above polar co-ordinates of System 45:

Angle: $\qquad$ -174.342870152° - 40.780000000° = - 215.122870152°

Distance: $\qquad$ 0.870263933 x 14 336 = 12 476.10374

The corresponding Cartesian co-ordinates are:

Y = 7 177.898952

X = - 10 204.45644

By adding these co-ordinates to the Østerlars co-ordinates, we find within the System 45 Bornholm - the theoretical co-ordinates of Olsker. But, taking into account the lateral reversal noted above, the X-co-ordinate must also reverse sign. The calculation gives:

> **Olsker:**
>
> Y = 56 658.79 + 7 177.898952 = **63 836.68895**
>
> X = 45 374.73 + 10 204.45644 = **55 579.18644**

4: **Nyker**

Using the same procedure as above, we find the co-ordinates to Point 108 Olsker:

Y = - √7:4 + 3:2 -√2 = - 0.747224265

X = - (√3:2 - √7: √3:4) = - 0.484144096

The corresponding polar co-ordinates are:

Angle $\qquad$ = - 122.9401469°

Distance = 0.890359258

Transferred to System 45 Bornholm:

Angle: $\qquad$ -122.9401469° - 40.7800000° = - 163.7201469°

Distance: $\qquad$ 0.890359258 x 14,336 = 12,764.19032

The corresponding Cartesian co-ordinates are

Y $\qquad$ = - 3 578.175203

X $\qquad$ = - 12 252.39637

The same procedure gives the theoretical co-ordinates to

> **Nyker:**
>
> Y = 56 658.79 - 3 578.175203 = **53 080.61480**
>
> X = 45 374.73 + 12 252.39637 = **57 627.12637**

5: **The Point C** (Point 111).

The Point C is purely theoretical - but is ruling the position of the churches of Olsker and Nyker as shown above. Point 111 has the following co-ordinates:

Y   = - (3 - √2) = - 1.585786438
X   = 0

The corresponding polar co-ordinates are:
Angle :   - 90°
Distance: 1.585786438

Transferred to System 45 Bornholm:
Angle: - 90° - 40.78° = - 130.78°
Distance: 1.585786438 x 14 336 = 22 733.83437

The corresponding Cartesian co-ordinates are:
Y   = - 17 214.58445
X   = - 14 848.74767

Same procedure as above gives the theoretical co-ordinates to

> **The Point C:**
> Y = 56 658.79 - 17 214.58446 = **39 444.20555**
> X = 45 374.73 + 14 848.74767 = **60 223.47767**

Note:

The table on page 177 illustrates how the real position of Olsker and the theoretical position of Olsker show by far the largest divergence within the geometry. It is accordingly of interest to see if the hypothetical position of Olsker could be confirmed by other indications of an intention to fulfil the geometrical pattern in accordance with our hypothesis.

It seems that the positions of the four round churches were deliberately chosen to indicate a "geometrical key". The hypothetical positions of the churches indicate the geometrical relationships necessary to construct the rest of the pattern - as will be shown.

If we suppose that the above was the intention in the layout of the four round churches - and if we further suppose that something interfered with the exact positioning of Olsker - then the logical thing to do would be to locate the church such that it would still indicate the most important of the geometric relationships.

It is possible to demonstrate, that this is exactly what the position of Olsker is doing. It is thus further confirmation of the presumed intent.

As we shall see in the following, there are two geometrical ratios in the key that have fundamental importance for the rest of the pattern. These ratios are:

1 : (3 - √2)

1 : (√7: √3:2)

Together with the Golden Section 1 : ([√5 + 1] : 2) and the ratios of the square and its diameter – **these are the only factors used in the whole geometry.**

The first of these ratios is connected to Point C – indicated by the intersection of the lines Nylars-Østerlars – and Olsker-Nyker (See Figure 3, p. 44).

The second of these ratios is indicated by the distance between Olsker-Nyker.

The position of Olsker is thus essential to both these ratios.

It must now be demonstrated that the actual position of Olsker – though not at the exact theoretical spot – is still capable of illustrating these two essential geometrical ratios with complete accuracy.

First it will be demonstrated, that a line through the actual positions of Olsker and Nyker is fixed upon the theoretical Point C.

This will be demonstrated through the calculation of the bearing from the theoretical Point C through Nyker - and the calculation of the bearing from the theoretical Point C through Olsker. If these two lines have the same bearing, it follows that a straight line through the actual churches of Olsker and Nyker will fix the theoretical Point C with 100 per cent accuracy.

A: The bearing of a line from C to actual Olsker

(The co-ordinates of the church spire of Olsker - the centre of the round church – will be found in the table at page NNN.)

Olsker:

Y   = 63 844.61

X   = 55 653.27

To calculate the required line, we subtract the co-ordinates of the Point C (shown above) from the co-ordinates of Olsker :

Y   = 63 844.61 - 39 444.20555   = 24 400.40445

X   = 55 653.27 - 60 223.47767   = - 4 570.20767

Our calculator gives us the bearing of this line: C - Olsker: 100.6086119°.

B: The bearing of a line from C to actual Nyker.

(The co-ordinates to the church spire of Nyker - the centre of the round church – will be found in the table at page 177.)

Nyker:

Y   = 53 086.37

X   = 57 665.44

To calculate the required line, we subtract the co-ordinates of the Point C (shown above) from the co-ordinates of Nyker:

Y   = 53 086.37 - 39 444.20555   = 13 642.16445
X   = 57 665.44 - 60 223.47767   = - 2 558.03767

The calculator gives the bearing of this line: C - Nyker: 100.6201902°.

The difference of the bearing from C to actual Olsker and from C to actual Nyker is: 100.6086119° - 100.6201902° = 0.01...°.

This means, that the actual positions of Olsker and Nyker are fixed upon the theoretical Point C with almost 100 per cent accuracy, despite the relatively much larger discrepancy between theoretical Olsker and actual Olsker. **QED.**

The distance from C to Olsker is approximately 25 kilometres. A discrepancy of 0.01 degrees at this distance represents about 5 metres. An observer, standing exactly at the point C and looking in the direction of Nyker and Olsker, would thus observe the spire of Olsker displaced from the spire of Nyker by 5 metres. Such a tiny displacement would only be observable through a powerful telescope. It demonstrates the astonishing accuracy of this geometry.

It will next be demonstrated, that the distance between actual Olsker and actual Nyker also illustrates the second profound geometrical ratio with complete accuracy.

Again we use the co-ordinates of actual Olsker and actual Nyker.
By subtracting the Nyker co-ordinates from the Olsker co-ordinates, we have the co-ordinates of the line actual Nyker - actual Olsker:

Y   =   63 844.61 - 53 086.37   =   10 758.24
X   =   55 653.27 - 57 665.44   =   - 2 012.17

The calculator gives the length of this line as:
Actual Nyker - actual Olsker: 10 944.79584 metres.

The geometrical ratio $\sqrt{7} : \sqrt{3} : 2 = 0.763762616$
This is to be multiplied by our unit 1 = 14 336 metres.
The length of the geometrical ratio is thus:
14 336 x 0.763762616 = 10 949.30086 metres.

The discrepancy between the theoretical distance Olsker-Nyker and the actual distance Olsker-Nyker is thus:
10 949.30 metres - 10 944.80 metres = 4.5 metres

This means that the actual positions of Olsker and Nyker indicate the theoretical distance with almost 100 per cent accuracy - despite the relatively much larger discrepancy between theoretical Olsker and actual Olsker. **QED.**

The above proves, that the profound geometrical ratios are still being illustrated with complete accuracy through the position of actual Olsker - despite the discrepancy between theoretical Olsker and actual Olsker. This provides further evidence of intent.

6: **Vestermarie**

(The following calculation is performed on Triangle ØL - NL - VE in diagram 6:)

Diagram 6

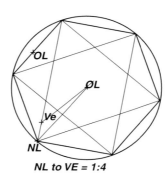

NL to VE = 1:4

The distance from Nylars to Vestermarie is 1:4 x Østerlars-Nylars. The angle Vestermarie-Nylars-Østerlars is 30°.

The formula used is the cosine relation:
$a^2 = b^2 + c^2 - 2 \times b \times c \times \cos A$
Thus:
$(\text{ØL to VE})^2 = 1^2 + (1{:}4)^2 - 2 \times 1 \times (1{:}4) \times \cos 30 =$
$1.0625 - 0.5 \times \cos 30 = 1.0625 - 0.5 \times 0.866025404 = 0.629487298$
ØL to VE $= \sqrt{0.629487298} = $ **0.793402356**

The formula used: $\sin C = c \times \sin A : a$
$\sin \text{VE-ØL-NL} = 0.25 \times \sin 30 : 0.793402356 =$
$0.25 \times 0.5 : 0.793402356 = 0.157549318$
Angle VE-ØL-NL = 9.064678386°

The above calculations give the following polar co-ordinates of Vestermarie
Angle $\quad = (- 90° - 9.064678386°) = - 99.064678386°$
Distance $= 0.793402356$

Transferred to System 45 Bornholm:
Angle   = - 99.064678386° - 40.78° = - 139.8446784°
Distance =   0.793402356 x 14 336 = 11 374.21618
which gives Cartesian co-ordinates:
Y   = - 7 334.798594
X   = - 8 693.303354
added to Østerlars (with X reversed sign) gives

Vestermarie:

Y = 56 658.79 - 7 334.798594 = **49 323.99141**

X = 45 374.73 + 8 693.303354 = **54 068.03335**

7: **Klemensker**

(The following calculations are performed on diagram 7)

Diagram 7

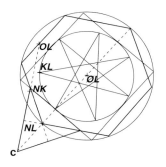

Klemensker is placed on a circle with centre in Østerlars and radius = 1: √2.
The angle from Østerlars-Klemensker to Østerlars-Nylars is 360° : 7.

Distance Østerlars - Klemensker: 1: √2 = 0.707106781
Angle to Y-axis: 360° : 7 = 51.42857143°

This gives the following polar co-ordinates of Klemensker.
Distance: 0.707106781
Angle: (- 90° - 51.42857143°) = -141.4285714°

Transferred to System 45 Bornholm:
Distance: 0.707106781 x 14 336 = 10 137.08282
Angle: -141.4285714° - 40.7800000° = - 182.2085714°
gives following Cartesian co-ordinates:
Y   =   390 6557768
X   =   - 10 129.55261

Reversed in X and added to Østerlars' co-ordinates this gives

---

Klemensker

Y = 56 658.79 + 390.6557768 = **57 049.44578**

X = 45 374.73 + 10 129.55261 = **55 504.28261**

8: **Christiansø**

(The following calculations are performed on Diagram 8)

Diagram 8

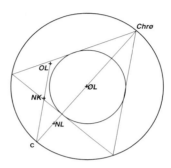

Christiansø is placed on the Y-axis (Østerlars-Nylars) – at a distance from Østerlars = √7: √3 The distance is illustrated by the geometrical key - being 2 x Olsker-Nyker.

Distance: √7 : √3 = 1.527525232
Angle (Y-axis): 90°

Transferred to System 45 Bornholm:
Distance: 1.527525232 x 14 336 = 21 898.60172
Angle: 90° - 40.78° = 49.22°

This gives following Cartesian co-ordinates:
Y = 16 582.127
X = 14 303.21018
reversed in X and added to Østerlars' co-ordinates this gives

---

Christiansø

Y = 56 658.79 + 16 582.127 = **73 240.917**

X = 45 374.73 - 14 303.21018 = **31 071.51982**

9: Rø

(The following calculations are performed on Diagram 9)

Diagram 9

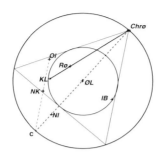

Rø is placed on a straight line between Klemensker and Christiansø - in the distance from Klemensker = 1:2 x Østerlars-Nylars

ØL to CHRØ = √7 : √3 = 1.527525232
ØL to KL = 1 : √2 = 0.707106781
The formula used is: $a^2 = b^2 + c^2 - 2$ x b x c x cosA
Thus:
(KL to CHRØ)^2 = 1.527525232^2 + 0.707106781^2 - 2 x 1.527525232 x 0.707106781
x cos (360 : 7 : 2 x 5) = 2.333333333 + 0.5 - 2.160246899 x cos 128.5714286 =
4.180225245
KL to CHRØ = √4.180225245 = 2.044559915

Distance CHRØ to RØ = (CHRØ to KL) - 1:2 = 2.044559915 - 0.5 = 1.544559915

Angle KL-CHRØ-ØL: (sin C = c x sin A : a)
sin KL-CHRØ-ØL = 0.707106781 x sin 128.5714286 : 2.044559915 =
0.270394787
KL-CHRØ-ØL = 15.68776033°
RØ-CHRØ-ØL = 15.68776033°

Using CHRØ as centre, RØ will give the following polar co-ordinates:
Angle: - 90° - 15.68776033° = -105.68776033°
Distance: 1.544559915
Transferred to System 45 Bornholm:
Angle: -105.68776033° - 40.7800000° = - 146.4677603°
Distance: 1.544559915 x 14 336 = 22 142.81094
which gives the following Cartesian co-ordinates:
Y = - 12 231.82419
X = - 18 457.69632

Adding these co-ordinates (with reversed X) to the CHRØ co-ordinates, we find

Rø
Y = 73 240.917 - 12 231.82419   = **61 009.09281**
X = 31 071.51982 + 18 457.69632 = **49 529.21614**

10 Bodilsker

(The following calculations are performed on diagram 10)

Diagram 10

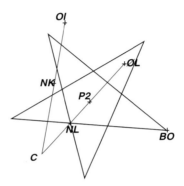

Bodilsker is placed on the vertex of a pentagram. The size of the pentagram is defined by the radius of the circumscribed circle - indicated by the geometrical key through the distance from Østerlars to the intersecting Point between the lines Østerlars-Nylars and Olsker-Nyker.

To find the radius, this distance (3 - $\sqrt{2}$) must be divided by the Golden Section. Thus the radius of the pentagram is (3 - $\sqrt{2}$) x ($\sqrt{5}$ - 1) : 2 = 0.980069917

The pentagram is placed such that one vertex is on the Y-axis ØL-NL - and the opposite intersection of two of the pentagram's sides is placed on Nylars. The vertex of Bodilsker is the first vertex clockwise after the vertex on the Y-axis.

Through calculation on the proportion of a pentagram we find the ratio between the radius, r, of a pentagram's circumscribed circle - and the part of the pentagram's diagonal equivalent to the line Nylars - Bodilsker =
NL to BO = $\sqrt{}$ ([5 - $\sqrt{5}$] : 2) x ([$\sqrt{5}$ + 1] : 2) x ([$\sqrt{5}$ - 1] : 2) x r = 1.175570505 x r

Since the radius of the Bodilsker pentagram is 0.980069917, it follows that the distance: NL to BO = 0.980069917 x 1.175570505 = 1.152141287
The angle: ØL-NL-BO = 54°

Using Nylars as centre and transferred to System 45, Bodilsker gives the following polar co-ordinates:

Distance: 1.152141287 x 14,336 = 16,517.09749

Angle: 90° - 54° - 40.78°   = - 4.78°

which gives the following Cartesian co-ordinates:

Y = - 1 376.369678

X = 16 459.65115

Adding these co-ordinates (with reversed X) to the Nylars co-ordinates, we find

---

Bodilsker

Y = 45 803.23969 - 1 376.369678 = **44 426.87001**

X = 54 738.37905 - 16 459.65115 = **38 278.7279**

---

11 **Point P 2**

(The following calculations are performed on Diagram 10 above. There is no diagram for Section 11).

P2 is the centre of the pentagram, calculated above. We find from the geometry that P2 is placed on the Y-axis.

From above we know:

r = 0.980069917

Calculation on the geometry of a pentagram gives us the ratio between r and that part of the line equivalent to Nylars-P2:

NL to P2 = $([\sqrt{5} - 1]:2)^2$ x r = 0.381966011 x 0.980069917 = 0.374353397

Angle (Y-axis): 90°

Using Nylars as centre and transferring to System 45 we find the following polar co-ordinates of P2:

Distance: 0.374353397 x 14 336 = 5 366.730301

Angle: 90° - 40.78° = 49.22°

which gives following Cartesian co-ordinates:

Y = 4 063.812135

X = 3 505.31383

Adding these (with reversed X) to the Nylars co-ordinates:

P2:

Y = 45 803.23969 + 4 063.812134 = **49 867.05182**

X = 54 738.37905 - 3 505.31383   = **51 233.06522**

---

12 **Ibsker**

(The following calculations are performed on the triangle P2-ØL-IB in Diagram 12)

Diagram 12

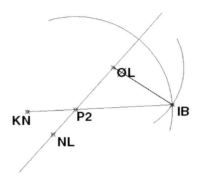

The position of Ibsker is defined by its distance from Østerlars and from P2. P2 is found through proportions indicated in the geometrical key. The distance from Østerlars is likewise indicated by the geometrical key = Olsker-Nyker.
ØL to IB = $\sqrt{7} : \sqrt{3} : 2$ = 0.763762616
P2 to IB = $(\sqrt{5} + 3) : 5$ = 1.047213596

P2 to ØL = (ØL to NY) - (NY to P2) = 1 - 0.374353397 = 0.625646603

Formula used: cos A = $(b^2 + c^2 - a^2) : 2 : b : c$
cos ØL-P2-IB =
(0.6256466032 + 1.0472135962 - 0.7637626162) : 2 : 0.625646603 : 1.047213596 =
 0.690458256
ØL-P2-IB = 46.33360522°

Using P2 as centre we find the following polar co-ordinates to Ibsker:
Distance: 1.047213596
Angle: 90° - 46.33360522° = 43.66639478°

Transferring these to System 45 Bornholm:
Distance: 1.047213596 x 14 336 = 15 012.85411
Angle: 43.66639478 - 40.78000000° = 2.88639478°
which gives the following Cartesian co-ordinates:
Y = 755.9840818
X = 14 993.80794

Adding these (with reversed X) to the co-ordinates of P2 we find

Ibsker

Y = 49 867.05182 + 755.9840818 = **50 623.0359**

X = 51 233.06522 - 14 993.80794 = **36 239.25728**

13 P1

(The following calculations are performed on Diagram 13)

Diagram 13

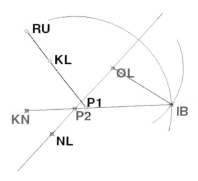

P1 is placed on the line P2-Ibsker - so that the distance
P1 to IB = ([$\sqrt{5}$ + 1] : 2) x 3:5 = 0.970820393

Using P2 as centre we find the following polar co-ordinates to P1:
Distance: (P2 to IB) - (P1 to IB) = 1.047213596 - 0.970820393 = 0.076393203
Angle: 43.66639478°

Transferring these to System 45 Bornholm:
Distance: 0.076393203 x 14 336 = 1 095.172958
Angle : 43.66639478° - 40.78000000° = 2.88639478°

Which gives the following Cartesian co-ordinates:
Y = 55.14829606
X = 1 093.783559

Adding these (with reversed X) to the P2 co-ordinate we find

P1

Y = 49 867.05182 + 55.14829605 = **49 922.20012**

X = 51 233.06522 - 1 093.783559 = **50 139.28166**

14 **Rutsker**

(The following calculations are performed on Diagram 14)

Diagram 14

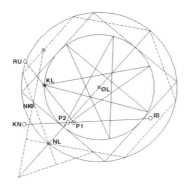

The position of Rutsker illustrates a means of constructing an approximate angle of 360° : 7.

Rutsker is placed at the circumference of the geometry's main circle (r = 1) – at an angle of - 90° - 69° from the X-axis.
Thus the polar co-ordinates are
Distance: 1
Angle: - 90° - 69° = - 159°

Transferred to System 45 Bornholm:
Distance: 1 x 14 336 = 14 336
Angle: - 159° - 40.78° = - 199.78°
which gives the following Cartesian co-ordinates:
Y = 4 851.438166
X = - 1 3490.161
added (with reversed X) to the co-ordinates of Østerlars gives :

Rutsker
Y = 56 658.79 + 4 851.438166 = **61 510.22817**
X = 45 374.73 + 1 3490.16100 = **58 864.891**

NOTE:

A line connecting Rutsker with P1 intersects the circle r = 1 : √2 approximately in Klemensker - indicating a method for the construction of an approximation to a seven pointed star.

The accuracy with which such an approximation is constructed can be calculated: (The following calculations are performed on diagram 14)

14a: P2-ØL-IB
(from above)
P2 to ØL = 0.625646603
P2 to IB = 1.047213596
ØL to IB = 0.763762616
ØL - P2 - IB = 46.33360522°
Formula used: sin C = (c x sin A) : a
Sin (P2 - ØL - IB) = (1.047213596 x sin 46.33360522) : 0.763762616 = 0.991833363
P2 - ØL - IB = 180° - 82.67250943° = 97.32749057°
P2 - IB - ØL = 180° - 97.32749057° - 46.33360522° = 36.33890421°

14b: P2 - ØL - P1
(from above)
P2 to ØL = 0.625646603
ØL - P2 - IB = 46.33360522°
(from definition:)
P2 to P1 = 2:5 x ([√5 + 1] : 2)² - 3:5 x ([√5 +1] : 2) = 0.076393202
Formula used: a² = b² + c² - 2 x b x c x cosA
(ØL to P1)² = 0.625646603² + 0.076393202² - 2 x 0.625646603 x 0.076393202 x cos 46.33360522 = 0.331268485
ØL to P1 = 0.57555928

Formula used: sin C = (c x sin A) : a
sin P2 - ØL - P1 = 0.076393202 x sin 46.33360522 : 0.57555928 = 0.096012215
P2 - ØL - P1 = 5.509581812°

14c: RU - ØL - P1
(from above)
ØL to RU = 1
ØL to P1 = 0.57555928
RU - ØL - P1 = (RU - Øl - NL) + (P2 - ØL - P1) = 69 + 5.509581812 = 74.50958181°

Formula used: $a^2 = b^2 + c^2 - 2bc \cos A$

(P1 to RU)^2 = 0.57555928^2 + 1^2 - 2 x 0.57555928 x 1 x cos 74.50958181 = 1.023830939

P1 to RU = 1.011845314

Formula used: sin C = (c x sin A) : a

sin (P1 - RU - ØL) = 0.57555928 x sin 74.50958181 : 1.011845314 = 0.548159049

P1 - RU - ØL = 33.24080745°

14d: RU-ØL-D

(from above)

(D is the intersection between the line P1-Rutsker and the Y-axis)

RU to ØL = 1

RU - ØL - D = 69°

D - RU - ØL = P1 - RU - ØL = 33.2408745°

RU - D - ØL = 180° - 69° - 33.2408745° = 77.7591255°

Formula used: a = (c x sin A) : sin C

ØL to D = 1 x sin 33.2408745 : sin 77.7591255 = 0.560912434

14e: KL' - ØL - D

(from above)

(KL' is the intersecting Point between the line P1-Rutsker and the circle r = 1 : √2.)

ØL - D - KL' = ØL-D-RU = 77.7591255°

ØL to D = 0.560912434

Øl to KL' = 1 : √2 = 0.707106781

Formula used: sin A = (a x sin C) : c

sin ØL - KL' - D = 0.560912434 x sin 77.7591255 : 0.707106781 = 0.775215218

ØL - KL' - D = 50.8245491°

KL' - ØL - D = 180 -77.7591255 - 50.8245491 = **51.4163254°**

Discrepancy from the centre angle in an equilateral seven pointed star:

(360° : 7) - 51.4163254° = 51.42857143° - 51.4163254° = 0.012246°

Klemensker (KL) marks the vertex of a seven-pointed star.

NOTE:

We know of no method to construct this Point geometrically. But since P1 and Rutsker (RU) (69 degrees = [90° - 72°] : 2 + 60°) - and the circle r = 1 : √2 - are all geometrically constructible, this means that KL' can be constructed. The geometry thus illustrates a way to construct an approximation to an angle of (360:7) degrees - with a deviation of little more than 1:100 degrees.

If such a construction was used in the lay out of Klemensker, the deviation from 100% accuracy - based on a radius of the circle = 14 336 : √2 = 10 137 metres - would only be 2.16... metres.

NOTE 2:

It is of interest to see with what accuracy the line through the actual churches of Rutsker and Klemensker indicates the theoretical Point P1 - which can be calculated:

From the table at page 177, we find the co-ordinates of

Actual Rutsker (the church tower):
Y = 61 535.30
X = 58 866.14

Actual Klemensker (the church tower):
Y = 57 063,72
X = 55 525.51

P1 (From above)
Y = 49 922.20012
X = 50 139.28166

The theoretical bearing of a line from P1 to Rutsker can be calculated from the above:
P1 to Rutsker = bearing (RU-D-ØL) + 90° = 77.7591255° + 90° = 167.7591255°
Transferred to System 45 Bornholm:
180° - 167.7591255° + 40.7800000° = **53.0208745°**.

By using the co-ordinates, we can calculate the bearing of the line P1-actual Klemensker - and the bearing of the line P1- actual Rutsker:

P1 - actual Klemensker
Y = 57 063,72 - 49 922.20012 = 7 141.51988
X = 55 525.51 - 50 139.28166 = 5 386.22834
Distance: 8 944.985295 metres
Bearing: 52.97592058°

P1 - actual Rutsker
Y = 61 535.30 - 49 922.20012 = 11 613.09988
X = 58 866.14 - 50 139.28166 = 8 726.858340
Distance: 14,526.6013 metres
Bearing: 53.07635578°

The deviation from perfect is thus:

Deviation: P1 - actual Rutsker = 53.0208745° - 53.07635578° = **- 0.055...°**
Deviation: P1 - actual Klemensker = 53.0208745° - 52.97592058° = **+ 0.045...°**

The theoretical line from P2 thus goes exactly between the two church towers - which demonstrates an incredible accuracy.

15: **Knudsker**

(The following calculations are performed on Diagram12.)

Diagram 12 (repeated)

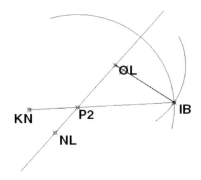

P2 to KN = 1 : 5 x (($\sqrt{5}$ + 1) : 2)^2 = 0.523606798

Bearing KN to P2 (to the X-axis) = 90° - (ØL-P2-IB) = 90° - 46.33360522° = 43.66639478°
Using P2 as centre and transferring to System 45, we find the following polar co-ordinates for Knudsker:
Distance: 0.523606798 x 14 336 = 7 506.427053
Angle: 43.66639478° - 40.78000000° + 180° = 182.88639478°

which gives the following Cartesian co-ordinates:
Y = - 377.9920303
X = -7 496.903969
Adding these (with reversed X) to the P2 co-ordinates, we find

Knudsker
Y = 49,867.05182 - 377.9920303 = **49,489.05979**
X = 51,233.06522 + 7,496.903969 = **58,729.96919**

NOTE

Knudsker, P2, P1 and Ibsker as previously demonstrated are all placed on a straight line. As we have seen from above, P1 is essential to the construction of an approximation to the angle (360:7) degrees. We shall see, that two more approximations are connected to this line.

The scaled length of the line - from Knudsker to Ibsker - is 3:5 x ([$\sqrt{5}$ + 1] : 2)^2 = 1.570820393 . This appears to be an approximation to pi:2 = 1.570796372 (one fourth of the circle (r = 1) circumference). The deviation from perfect is (1.570820393 - 1.570796372) = 0.000024066.

Diagram 15

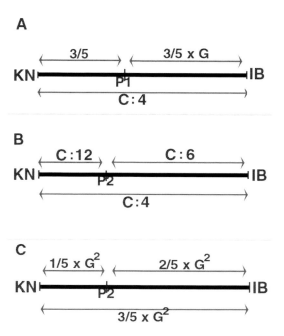

P2 divides this approximation into 1:3 and 2:3 - thus marking the length of the same approximation pi:3 and pi:6 (one sixth and one twelfth of the circle circumference). The line is thus marking the length of an arc connected respectively to the square (pi:4), the six pointed star (pi:3) and the twelve divisions of the circle (pi:6) - the most common divisions of the circle)

P1 divides this line in the Golden Section Division ($\sqrt{5}$ + 1) : 2.
The third approximation, connected to this line, will be demonstrated in the following .

16: **Povlsker**

(The following calculations are performed on the triangle P1-IB-PV in Diagram 16)

Diagram 16

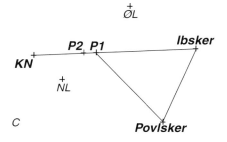

Povlsker is placed at a distance from P1 equal to the distance from P1 to Ibsker - and at a distance from Ibsker equal to half the distance from Ibsker to Knudsker.

IB to PV = 1 : 2 x (IB to KN) = 1:2 x (3:5 + 3:5 x (($\sqrt{5}$ + 1) : 2)) = 0.785410197
P1 to PV = P1 to IB = 3:5 x (($\sqrt{5}$ + 1) : 2) = 0.970820393
Formula used: cos A = (b^2 + c^2 - a^2) : 2 : b : c
Cos IB-P1-PV = (0.970820393^2 + 0.970820393^2 - 0.785410197^2) : 2 : 0.970820393
: 0.970820393 = 0.672745751
IB-P1-PV = 47.72066147°

Using P1 as centre, this gives the following polar co-ordinates of Ibsker:
Distance: 0.970820393
Angle: 43.6663948° - 47.72066147° = -4.05426667°

Transferring to System 45 Bornholm:
Distance: 0.970820393 x 14 336 = 13 917.68115
Angle: -4.0542663° - 40.78000000° = -44.83426667°

which gives the following Cartesian co-ordinates
Y = - 9 812.778758
X = 9 869.712339

Adding these (with reversed X) to the co-ordinates of P1 we find

> **Povlsker**
> **Y** = 49 922.20012 - 9 812.778758 = **40 109.42136**
> **X** = 50 139.28166 - 9 869.712339 = **40 269.56932**

NOTE:

The use of the particular geometrical ratios, demonstrated by the position of Povlsker, makes good sense, because it seems to belong to an (obviously secret) knowledge of geometry. Within the paradigm of medieval thinking, geometry was considered to have religious importance. It is therefore reasonable to imagine, that certain geometrical solutions to 'divine mysteries' – that is geometrical approximations to irrational and transcendental configurations – would have been considered confidential to an initiated group of religious people.

A knowledge of sacred geometrical ratios could safely have been used in the layout of the Bornholm geometry since no one outside the initiated group would ever have been able to discover it.

Here it will be demonstrated, that the geometrical ratios, used in the Bornholm geometry through the position of Povlsker - illustrate a means to construct an approximation to 1: 9 of a degree (and thus makes it possible to construct 1:3 of a degree - and 1 degree). The accuracy of this approximation is extremely good.

17 **Approximation to 1: 9 degrees**

(The following calculations are performed on three triangles: P2 - ØL - IB, P1 - IB - PV and P2 - P1 - PV - shown in Diagram 17)

Diagram 17

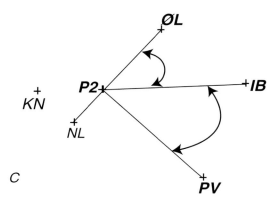

IB - P2 - ØL (from 12) = 46.33360522°
IB - P1 - PV (from 16) = 47.72066147°

P2 - P1 - PV = 180° - (IB - P1 - PV) = 132.2793385°
P1 to PV = 3:5 x ([√5 + 1] : 2) = 0.970820393
P2 to P1 = 2:5 x ([√5 +]) : 2)2 - 3:5 x ([√5 + 1] : 2) = 0.076393202
Formula used: $a^2 = b^2 + c^2 - 2bc \cos A$
(P2 to PV)^2 =
0.9708203932 + 0.0763932032 - 2 x 0.970820393 x 0.076393203 x cos 132.2793385 = 1.048115294
P2 to PV = √1.048115294 = 1.023775021

Formula used: sin C = (c x sin A) : a

sin (P1 - P2 - PV) = 0.970820393 x sin 132.2793385 : 1.023775021 = 0.701603871
P1 - P2 - PV = 44.55582485°

(IB - P2 - ØL) - (P1 - P2 - PV) =
A = 46.33360522 - 44.55582485 = **1.777780368°**

Deviation from 16 : 9 degrees:
16 : 9 - 1.77780368 = 1.777777778 - 1.777780368 = **0.000002591°**

16 = 2 x 2 x 2 x 2. Thus - through division of 16 : 9 can be constructed the approximation:
= (1.777780386 : 16) = **0.111111273**

Deviation from 1 : 9 degrees:
1 : 9 - 0.111111273 = **0.000000162°**

From this we find that by using the above approximation to 1: 9 degrees - and dividing a circle into 9 x 360 such equal pieces, the total deviation from a perfect circle would be:
0.000000162 x 9 x 360 = 0.0005 of a degree!

NOTE

There is an inherent error connected to calculations with sines and cosines when performed in a calculator.

Such an error can be estimated as having no importance in relation to the calculations of the positions of the churches by use of co-ordinates as the error will not significantly alter the calculated positions.

However, the error may have marginal influence on the calculations of the approximations.

It has not been possible within the frame of this investigation to establish if such an influence is significant.

COMPARATIVE ANALYSIS OF THE ACTUAL AND THEORETICAL CO-ORDINATES TO THE MEDIEVAL CHURCHES AT BORNHOLM

In the following table, the official Danish government land surveyor's co-ordinates of the church towers are compared with the theoretical positions suggested by the geometry.

X co-ordinates are calculated from east to west, Y co-ordinates from south to north.

Thus the subtraction of the surveyor's X co-ordinates from the theoretical X co-ordinates, provides the displacement, in metres, of the theoretical point in an east/west direction.

Likewise, the subtraction of the surveyor's Y co-ordinates from the theoretical Y co-ordinates gives the displacement, in metres, in a north/south direction.

Discussion:

The actual co-ordinates of Point Christiansø are listed only to demonstrate where the medieval compass in the rock would have been in relation to the position of the Store Tårn in 1684. The need for building material in connection with the

Church	Surveyor's co-ordinate to church tower		Theoretical co-ordinate		Fixed Point to Theoretical Point in metres.	
	Y	X	Y	X	Y North = + South = -	X West = + East = -
Østerlars	56 658.79	45 385.33	56 658.79	45 374.73	0	-10.6
Nylars	45 803.09	54 748.17	45 803.23969	54 738.37905	+0.15	-9.79
Olsker	63 844.61	55 653.27	63 836.68895	55 579.18644	-7.92	-74.08
Nyker	53 086.37	57 665.44	53 080.6148	57 627.12637	-5.76	-38.31
Point C			39 444.20555	60 223.47767		
Vestermarie	49 331.53	54 112.87	49 323.99141	54 068.03335	-7.54	-44.84
Klemensker	57 063.72	55 525.51	57 049.44578	55 504.28261	-14.27	-21.23
Point Christiansø	73 299.55 (StoreTårn)	31 10-2.51 (Store Tårn)	73 240.-917	31 071.-51982	-58.63	-30.99
Rø	61 011.26	49 564.33	61 006.09281	49 529.21614	-5.17	-35.11
Bodilsker	44 474.00	38 287.27	44 426.87001	38 278.7279	-47.13	-8.54
Point P-2			49 867.05182	51 233.06522		
Ibsker	50 624.19	36 258.57	50 623.0359	36 239.25728	-1.15	-19.31
Point P-1			49 922.20012-	50 139.28166-		
Rutsker	61 535.30	58 866.14	61 510.22817	58 864.891	-25.07	-1.25
Knudsker	49 484.62	58 767.81	49 489.05978	58 729.96919	+4.43	-37.84
Povlsker	40 110.82	40 300.32	40 109.42136	40 269.56932	-1.43	-30.75

fortification of the tiny island in 1684 led to the destruction of the rock-compass.

As they do not form part of our analysis, the Christiansø co-ordinates are excluded from the following calculations.

When we analyse the rest of the co-ordinates illustrating the difference between actual and theoretical - and exclude Østerlars and Nylars - we find the average numerical distance from actual to theoretical position:
Y = (119.87 : 10) = 11.99 metres
X = (311.26 : 10) = 31.13 metres

A look at the calculated X-co-ordinates shows that they are all negative. And so they should be!

This is because the actual co-ordinates are to the tower - the westernmost part of the church - while the most important part of the church, from the religious point of view, is located to the east.

If we assume that the altar, on average, is placed 20 metres due east of the church tower, we can make the following compensation to the average divergence in the X-co-ordinates:
X = 31.13 - 20 = 11.13 metres

Which means, when we compare the average divergence:
Y = 11.99 metres
X = 11.13 metres
But in fact, it is better than that.

The X co-ordinates shows one that stands out: Olsker : - 74.08.
This is about twice as much as the nearest other example, which is Vestermarie: -44.84
But analysis has shown Vestermarie to be without divergence.
The anomaly seems to be due to the construction of the new church – *(see Chapter Four)*.

Our hypothesis is that Olsker could not be placed exactly at the required location.

When the Y-co-ordinates are examined, a similarly anomalous co-ordinate can be identified: Bodilsker: Y = - 47.13.

This co-ordinate is also nearly twice as much as the next nearest divergence: Rutsker : Y = - 25.07.

Bodilsker, however, provides a perfect explanation for this divergence. The theoretical Point - the vertex of a pentagram - was not meant to be inside the church. Instead it is marked with absolute precision by a stone in the watch-tower to the south of the church (See Chapter Five).

From the above, it seems more reasonable to look at the churches one by one when we try to estimate the precision of their layout in accordance with the geometry. The following churches have the theoretical Point within the church itself:
(Østerlars - Nylars) - Vestermarie - Ibsker.

Rø might have been exactly positioned. The theoretical Point is less than 10 metres due east of the apse of the present church. But Rø has been rebuilt. The present church may have been located to the west of the original building - as it has already been possible to demonstrate was the case with Vestermarie (See Chapter Four).

Klemensker may also have been exactly positioned. Today, the point is 5 metres south of the church-wall - exactly reflecting the position of the altar inside the church. But Klemensker is also a new building - and it may not have been constructed precisely on the foundations of the old church. It may have been relocated slightly to the north. Since Klemensker is placed on a natural hill, the topography may also have limited the possibilities.

This problem is even more clearly evident in the case of **Rutsker.** The theoretical Point is found about 20 metres south of the southern wall of the church. Today, several hundred cubic metres of soil have been laid south of the church to extend and level the churchyard. But at the time of the original construction, the terrain had a steep slope at the theoretical Point. The church could simply not have been moved further south without an enormous expenditure of labour.

The topography of the landscape plays an important role throughout. The line P1 - Klemensker - Rutsker goes directly from hill top to hill top. P1 is the highest Point of the island. It certainly seems – and perhaps not surprisingly - that when the geometry was first laid out, the specific topographical features of the island affected the design decisions which were being made,.

Olsker - as noted – has by far the greatest inaccuracy. It is our hypothesis that something made it necessary to move the church. As we shall see in the following, this may even have necessitated other apparent inaccuracies.

Nyker is placed such, that a line through Olsker and Nyker is aligned on the geometry's important theoretical Point C - as explained above. This is only possible through an equivalent slight displacement of the church in a due westerly direction - exactly as is the case for the actual position.

The last two churches - Knudsker and Povlsker - are also placed due west of their theoretical points. When their positions are examined in relation to Olsker - Nyker - we find something remarkable.

Knudsker has its theoretical point some 15 metres due east of the church apse. Its position in regard to the theoretical point is thus analogous to that of Nyker - although we do not know of any particular geometrical link which can be demonstrated by the relation between Knudsker and Nyker. It is, nevertheless, noteworthy - as we shall see in the following.

Povlsker is the strangest of them all and is the only one of the mediaeval churches to be built without a western tower. However, the surveyor's co-ordinates fix the location of the strange cubic watch-tower, which lies some 25 metres *east* of the church.

The theoretical point is due east of this tower. But here we have a problem similar to that which we encountered at Rutsker. The tower sits at the easternmost edge of a small, natural hill top. East of the tower the terrain slopes steeply. The geometry seems to be acting as if this eastern tower was indeed a western tower – but lying in relation to a phantom church on the inconveniently precipitous slope of the hillside.

This thought is accentuated by the strange connection between the four last mentioned churches: Olsker, Nyker, Knudsker and Povlsker. All the mediaeval churches in this analysis are part of the same geometry. But these four churches seems to have a specific connection.

It has been demonstrated how a relocation of Olsker is geometrically connected to a relocation of Nyker. It seems that Knudsker and Povlsker likewise are connected to the relocation of Nyker, which can be illustrated through a simple analysis.

We compare the actual distances and angles between the churches with the theoretical ones. The surveyor's co-ordinates of the church towers are used as the actual. The co-ordinates of the corresponding theoretical points are those calculated above.

Povlsker - Nyker
Actual:
Y = 53 086.37 - 40 110.82 = 12 975.55
X = 57 665.44 - 40 300,32 = 17 365.12
Distance: 21 677.46042 Angle: 36.7677892°
Theoretical:
Y = 53 080.61480 - 40 109.42136 = 12 971.19344
X = 57 627.12637 - 40 269.56932 = 17 357.55705
Distance: 21 668.79429 Angle: 36.77053141°

Discrepancy from theoretical in:
Distance: 21 677.46042 - 21 668.79429   **= 8.67 metres**
Angle: 36.7677829° - 36.77053141°   **= 0.0027°!**

Povlsker - Knudsker
Actual:
Y = 49 484.62 - 40 110.82 = 9 373,8
X = 58 767.81 - 40 300,32 = 18 467.49
Distance: 20 710.29486 Angle: 26.9116145°
Theoretical:
Y = 49 489.05978 - 40 109.42136 = 9.379.63842
X = 58 729.96919 - 40 269.56932 = 18 460.39987
Distance: 20 706.61682 Angle: 26.93489975°
Discrepancy from theoretical in:
Distance: 20 710.29486 - 20 706.61682   **= 3.68 metres**
Angle: 26.9116145 - 26.93489975   **= - 0.023°**

Knudsker - Nyker

Actual:

Y = 53 086.37 - 49 484.62 = 3 601.75

X = 57 665.44 - 58 767.81 = - 1 102.37

Distance: 3 766.672627 Angle: 107.0175216°

Theoretical:

Y = 53 080.61480 - 49 489.05978 = 3 591.55502

X = 57 627.12637 - 58 729.96919 = - 1 102.84282

Distance: 3 757.06398 Angle: 107.0699184°

Discrepancy from theoretical in:

Distance: 3 766.672627 - 3 757.06398   **= 9.61 metres**

Angle: 107.0175216° - 107.0699184°   **= - 0.052°**

It should be remembered that aerial photographs seem to have identified a pre-existing building close to the emplacement of 'theoretical Olsker'. (See p. 55)

The hypothesis, that Olsker was relocated due to something which made it impossible to place it at its exact theoretical spot, seems to be further corroborated through this analysis. It must be assumed that it was important for this particular part of the geometry to be indicated with the utmost precision.

We have already argued that Nyker, as well as Olsker, had to relocated. From the above analysis it seems that there is a further specific geometrical relation between the churches of Nyker, Knudsker and Povlsker, since their actual relative locations (from tower to tower) have practically no divergence from their hypothetical relation in distance and angle, although there is a small divergence from the theoretical point to the actual church as shown above.

In particular this analysis corroborates the argument, that the position of the watch-tower of Povlsker church, which lacks a western tower, was meant symbolically to indicate a phantom church located on the steep eastern slope of the hillside.

The curiosity of these geometric relationships may help in an understanding of how the system was measured out and constructed. It may also be hinting at something else in the geometry which is of importance and which, thus far, we have not been able to uncover.

There would seem to be additional layers of meaning and significance in these extraordinary labours which, as yet, elude our grasp.

*   *   *

Even with the remaining uncertainties, the findings demonstrate an extreme and undeniable skill. They can no longer be considered the results of haphazard chance. Certainly, the precision shown should have laid to rest any remaining claims that we have simply imposed an imaginary design upon the landscape. It is our hope that the accuracy of the measures will spur further investigation by those competent in the mathematics and geometry.

The Bornholm Layout was created with extreme care and with an obviously serious intent. As more facts are laid bare, fantasies will fade and knowledge will grow. We have uncovered an ancient wonder. It is a work of genius – displaying enlightenment, erudition and wisdom. But the discovery is not enough. Now we must try to understand what those forgotten masters were handing on to us. The prize may be greater than we know.

CHRONOLOGY

BC

c.1350 Ark of the Covenant and Laws of God given to Moses on Mount Sinai.

c.900   King David brings the Ark to Jerusalem.

c.870   King Solomon builds the Temple.

c.700   King Hezekiah tunnels aqueduct through Mount Sion.

586   Nebuchadnezzar, King of Babylon, conquers Jerusalem.

      Hebrews taken in captivity to Babylon.

      The Ark of the Covenant disappears.

586 – 538 Old Testament written during 'Babylonian Captivity'.

AD

326   Helena, mother of Emperor Constantine, identifies the Holy Sepulchre.

679   Dagobert II (Merovingian King) assassinated.

1060   Godefroi de Bouillon born.

1090   St Bernard of Clairvaux born.

1095   Council of Clermont - Pope Urban II preaches crusade.

1098   Cistercians founded in Citeaux.

1099   Capture of Jerusalem – Godefroi de Bouillon offered the Crown.

c.1100   Eskil (Danish Archbishop) born.

1100   Death of Godefroi de Bouillon. Baudouin accepts Crown of Jerusalem.

1113   St Bernard joins the Cistercians.

1115   St Bernard founds Clairvaux.

1118 / 1119 Templars founded in Jerusalem.

1128   Council of Troyes – St Bernard becomes 'Protector' of the Templars.

      Absalon (Danish Bishop) born.

1131   Valdemar the Great, King of Denmark, born.

1137   Eskil becomes Archbishop.

1153   Bertrand de Blanchefort becomes Templar Grand Master.

      Death of Bernard of Clairvaux.

1154   Nicholas Breakspear elected as Pope Adrian IV.

1159   Death of Pope Adrian IV.

      Election of Pope Alexander III.

1164   Fulco appointed Bishop of Estonia.

1170   Death of Bertrand de Blanchefort.

1177   Archbishop Eskil retires to Clairvaux.

1181   Death of Pope Alexander III.

      Archbishop Eskil dies at Clairvaux.

1182   Death of Valdemar the Great, King of Denmark.

1200	Bishop Albert founds Riga monastery.
1201	Death of Bishop Absalon.
1202	The Knights of the Sword, (offshoot of the Templars), founded in Riga by the Cistercian, Theoderic van Treiden. Valdemar II became Danish king.
1211	Theoderic van Treiden appointed Bishop of Estonia.
1305	Election of Bertrand de Goth as Pope Clement V.
1307	King Philippe le Bel of France orders arrest of Knights Templar.
1314	Jacques Burgundius de Molay, Templar Grand Master, burned in Paris.
	Death of Pope Clement V.
	Death of King Philippe le Bel.
1852	Bérenger Saunière born.
1885	Bérenger Saunière appointed priest of Rennes-le-Château.
1891	Supposed discovery of Rennes-le-Château parchments.
c1900	Valter Juvelius, Finnish librarian, discovers cipher in Old Testament.
1909 –1911	Johan Millén leads English archaeological expedition in Jerusalem.
1917	Death of Bérenger Saunière.
1953	Death of Marie Denarnaud.

BIBLIOGRAPHY

Knytlinge Saga, Copenhagen, 1977.

Danmarks Kirker, Bornholm, Copenhagen 1954.

De danske Kirker, Bind 19, Copenhagen 1970.

Arcons, C. d', *Du flux et reflux de la mer... Paris,* 1667.

Baigent, M., Leigh, R., Lincoln, H., *The Holy Blood and the Holy Grail,* Jonathan Cape, London, 1982.

Baigent, M., Leigh, R., Lincoln, H., *The Messianic Legacy,* Jonathan Cape, London, 1986.

Beckmann, P., *A history of Pi,* New York, 1971

Benninghoven, F. *Der Orden der Schwertbrüder,* Böhlau Verlag, 1956.

Berriman, A.E. *Historical Metrology,* Dent, London, 1953

Bidstrup, M., *Bornholms Middelalderlige Kirker,* Bornholmske Samlinger 7, 1912

Boudet, H., *La Vraie Langue Celtique,* Belisane, Nice, 1984.

Charpentier, L.. *Les mystères de la cathédrale de Chartres,* Laffont, 1966.

Connor, R.D., *Weights & Measures of England,* HMSO Books, Norwich, 1987.

Drosnin, M.. *The Bible Code,* Weidenfeld & Nicolson, 1997.

Flinders Petrie, W.M., *The Great Pyramid,* London, 1893.

Frölén, H. F., *Nordens befästa rundkyrkor,* Stockholm, 1891.

Fulcanelli, *Le Mystère des Cathédrales,* Paris, 1964.

Gardner, L., *The Bloodline of the Holy Grail,* Element Books,1996.

Gildas, M., *St Bernard of Clairvaux,* Catholic Encyclopaedia, 1913.

Gill, D., *Geology of the City of David* in Monographs of the Institute of Archaeology,
   Hebrew University, 1996.

Haagensen, E., *Bornholms Mysterium,* Bogans Forlag, Denmark, 1993.

Holm, H.J., *Bornholms Aeldgamle Kirkebygninger,* Copenhagen, 1878.

Hørby, K., *Bornholm in the Baltic during the Crusading period,* Copenhagen, 1992.

Johansen, P., *Die Estlandsliste des Liber Census Daniae,* Copenhagen, 1933.

Johansen, P., *Nordische Mission, Revals Gründung und die Schwedensiedlung in Estland,* Stockholm, 1951.

Jørgensen, J.A., *Bornholms Historie,* Rønne, 1900.

Kjellson, H., *Försvunden Teknik,* 1961 (Republished Valentin Vorlag, 1995).

Kofoed, A.E., *Christiansøs Historie,* Rønne, 1984.

Körner, K., *Die Templerregel,* Jena, 1902.

Lincoln, H., *The Holy Place,* Jonathan Cape, London, 1991.

Lincoln, H., *Key to the Sacred Pattern,* Windrush Press, 1997.

Millén, J., *På rätta vägar,* Stockholm, 1917.

Mogstad, S.V., *Frimureri,* Universitetsforlaget, Oslo, 1994.

Morris, R., *Churches in the Landscape,* Dent, London, 1989.

Nørlund, P.E., *Trelleborg,* Copenhagen, 1948.

Poulsen, H., *Den Store Pyramide,* Copenhagen, 1980.

Saxo Grammaticus, *Gesta Danorum,* Copenhagen, 1924

Schmidt, L., *Geschichten der deutschen Stämme,*

Schonfield, H., *The Essene Odyssey,* Element Books, 1984.

Séde, G. de, *Le Trésor Maudit,* Editions J'ai Lu, Paris, 1968.

Simson, O. von, *The Gothic Cathedral,* New York, 1956.

Smith, J.R., *From Plane to Spheroid,* Landmark, California, 1986.

Stiesdal, H., *Gravningsrapport til Nationalmuseet,* July 1955.

Strange, J., *Theology & Politics in Architecture & Iconography,* Aarhus University Press, 1991.

Thom, A., *The Geometry of Megalithic Man,* Mathematical Gazette, 1961.

Vincent, H., *Underground Jerusalem,* London, 1911.

Wienberg, J., *Bornholms kirker i den ældre Middalalder,* Hikuin 12, 1986.

Wivel, M., *Bornholms Runde Kirker og Tempelridderne,* Bornholmske Samlinger, 1989.

Wood, D., *Genisis,* Baton Press, Tunbridge Wells, 1985.

Zuckerman, A.J., *A Jewish Princedom in Feudal France,* New York, 1972.

Appendix
CORVUS – THE RAVEN
(see footnote page 44)

It is certainly possible to make a purely subjective comparison between the layout of the round churches of Bornholm and the constellation of Corvus, the Raven.

Figure 24

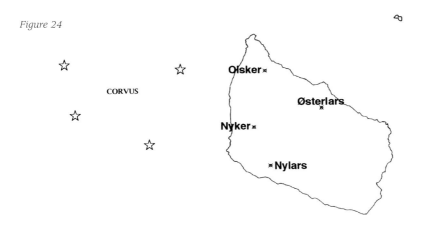

That some man-made structures may have been positioned in order to reflect an observed pattern in the stars is, of course, not an original suggestion. The most well-known recent example is that made by Robert Bauval and Adrian Gilbert in their book *The Orion Mystery* (Heinemann, 1994), in which the authors see the configuration of the constellation Orion mirrored in the pyramids of Giza. Their theory can be supported by the fact that Orion was linked to Osiris, who played such a major part in the religious cults surrounding the Pharaoh.

A less well-known example of such a suggestion was made by Louis Charpentier in *Les mystères de la cathédrale de Chartres* (Laffont 1966). Here, the layout of the constellation Virgo – the Virgin – is apparently displayed in an enormous pattern spread across northern France. It is formed by the cathedrals of Bayeux, Amiens, Reims, Chartres and Evreux.

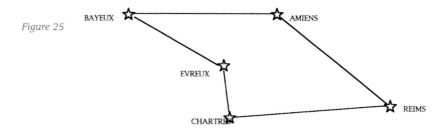

Figure 25

Each of these cathedrals is dedicated to *Notre Dame* – the Virgin Mother of God. Again there is the suggestion of a link with the cults of Ancient Egypt. The Virgin, *Notre Dame* (and particularly the evocative 'Black Virgins'), are frequently linked with the much older worship of Isis, sister and wife of Osiris.[55]

The constellation Corvus, the Raven, also has interesting mythological associations – but, this time, they are Greek. According to legend, the god Apollo commanded the Raven to bring water in a *crater* (a cup or goblet – faint echo of the Grail). But the greedy bird was distracted and wasted its time gorging upon figs. In order to provide an excuse and alibi, the raven gathered up Hydra, the water snake, in its claws and flew back to Apollo, claiming that the serpent was the cause of his delay. But Apollo was enraged and hurled all three, the Raven, the *Crater* and the Hydra, into the heavens where they were transformed into a group of constellations. Significantly, all three of these elements are important symbols in the ancient science of alchemy, which blends religion, philosophy and astrology.

The Raven, being black, symbolises *nigredo* – the first stage of the alchemical process. This is the stage of corruption and decay, necessitating change. In some texts, this stage can also be symbolised by a skull. The skull and cross-bones flag – now associated so strongly with piracy, has been claimed to find its origin in the flag borne by the ships of the Knights Templar. The same image is also strongly linked with Freemasonry. Thus, tenuously, can the links be forged. The skull and the cross as a representation of the decay of the material world, resting upon the Cross of Christ, becomes the hope of the human spirit for liberation from the bonds of matter.

From the *nigredo* stage of the Raven, the alchemist moves on to *preparatio*, the production of the raw material for his process, which must then be sublimated. This leads to the eventual change to *materia tertia*, which requires purification – *purificatio*. And this is symbolised by the cup or chalice: the *crater*.

[55] Charpentier also makes reference to a group of Benedictine abbeys which, seemingly, depict *Ursa Major* – the Great Bear.

Through further sublimation and distillation the alchemist finally produces the *lapis philosophorum* – the Philosopher's Stone. This stage is also known as *coniunctio* – the final aim of the alchemist. Among the symbols for this stage is a snake, *Ouroboros,* devouring its own tail. This snake is known to Nordic mythology as *Midgaardsormen* which surrounds the globe in its habitation, the ocean. A water-snake : Hydra.

The raven also plays an important symbolic role in the cult of the ancient Roman religion known as the Mithraic Mysteries. The central icon of the cult, found in all temples dedicated to Mithras, is the *tauroctony* or 'bull-slaying', in which the god is shown in the act of killing a bull. In this scene, Mithras is always accompanied by a dog, a scorpion, a snake and a raven. The four creatures are all symbols of constellations.

Temples of Mithras were widely spread throughout the Roman Empire. The Roman army seems to have been the major propagator of the cult, which had a particular appeal to the soldiery. The Mithraic Mysteries demonstrate many interesting parallels with the specific form of Christianity followed by another military group, the Knights Templar, though these lie beyond the scope of this book. It must suffice to sense, yet again, the unexpected scent of the possible link.

Yet another tantalising such possibility is to be found with the Emperor Constantine, who built the Church of the Holy Sepulchre, where the Templars allegedly took their original vows He, too, as a soldier of Rome, followed the Mithraic cult and was not finally baptised into the Christian faith until he lay upon his death-bed. Even more curious is one of the fragments which surfaced from Sverre Dag Mogstad's delving into the archives of Swedish Freemasonry. Not only did he encounter the frequently made claim of the masons to be descended from the Knights Templar. He also quotes their claim that Constantine the Great was among their Grand Masters.[56]

As with other such purely subjective readings of evidence, it is by no means difficult to construct a tempting connection between the terrestrial layout of the churches of Bornholm and the heavenly symbol of the Raven. Many people delight in clinging to such possibilities as if they were proven facts.

However, it is impossible to prove, beyond any reasonable doubt, that the pattern observed in the church layout is evidence of an intention to reflect the disposition of the stars. The number of possible star patterns far exceeds the probabilities of finding a coincidental matching in a layout on the ground. Even when it is possible to strengthen the possibility with a connected legend or cult, a *proof* of intention demands much more than a mere similarity in lay-out. On the other hand, lack of an absolute accuracy in the matching patterns does not *disprove*

---

[56] *Frimureri,* Sverre Dag Mogstad, Universitetsforlaget, Oslo 1994.

such a possibility, since we cannot know what degree of exactitude was, or could have been, employed in the construction. The suggestion is briefly explored here, in acknowledgement that the suggestion has been made. It is therefore worth recording, if only for the light which such thinking may shed upon some of the interpretations of the otherwise apparently straightforward facts.

INDEX

Aakirke, 143
Abraham, 96
Absalon, 31, 32, 36, 183, 184
Adrian IV, see Breakspear, Nicholas
Alexander III, Pope, 34 - 36, 92, 183
Alexandria, 20
Alfred the Great, King, 10
Alvastra, 33
Amiens, 187, 188
Anastasius IV, Pope, 34
Anna, 89
Apollo, 188
Arcadia, Shepherds of, 64
Archimedes, 20
Argo, see Argonauts,
Argos, see Argonauts,
Argonauts, 17
Arimathea, Joseph of, 24, 27, 90, 91, 92, 93, 94
Ark of the Covenant, 28, 98, 99, 101, 106,
    133 - 135, 183
Arkona, 15
Atbash cipher, 99
Athlit, 14
Attila, King, 11

Baigent, Michael, 5
Baltic Sea, 3, 8, 10, 12, 13, 15, 22, 30, 31, 33,
    35, 36, 39, 43, 62, 78, 135 - 137, 185
Baphomet, 79, 130
Barbarossa, Frederick, 33, 34
Barcelona, 73
Bauval, Robert, 187
Bayeux, 187, 188
Becket, Thomas à, 34
Benedictines, 188
Bernard, Saint, 16, 17, 28 - 30, 32 - 35, 38,
    39, 78, 87, 94, 130, 133 - 137, 183, 185
Bible, 24, 91, 96, 99, 100, 185
Bidstrup, Mathias, 15, 185
Black Virgin, 188
Blanchefort (mountain), 69, 70
Blanchefort, Bertrand de, 33, 34, 36, 72, 87,
    130, 133, 136, 137, 183, 184

Bodilsker, 38, 66, 67, 164, 165, 177, 178
Bøllshavn, 63
Bornholm, 4 - 6, 8 -16, 20, 22, 29 - 31,
    38 - 42, 46 - 49, 52, 54 - 59, 61 - 64, 66,
    67, 69, 72 - 74, 76, 77, 79, 87, 88, 105,
    109, 115, 117, 118, 120, 121, 123, 124,
    126, 127, 130, 132, 133, 135, 137, 139,
    143, 153, 155 - 157, 161, 174, 176, 182,
    185 - 187, 189
Boudet, Abbé Henri, 70 - 72, 75, 83, 87, 185
Bourgogne, see Burgundy, Dukedom of,
Breakspear, Nicholas, 33, 34, 183
Bremen, 31, 34
Burgendaland, 10
Burgunda, 10
Burgunderholm, 10
Burgunderland, 10
Burgundy, Dukedom of, 10, 11, 17, 18, 29, 30,
    34, 78, 133, 134

Cambridge, 20, 61
Canseliet, Eugène, 17
Canterbury, 34
Canute, see Knud,
Champagne, Count of, 29, 78
Charles XIII, King of Sweden, 26, 87, 92, 94,
    95, 133
Charles XVI Gustav, King, 95
Charpentier, Louis, 16, 17, 57, 78, 185, 187, 188
Chartres, 16, 17, 57, 78, 185, 187, 188
Childeric, 134
Christ, Jesus, 12, 15, 24, 25, 27, 39, 78, 88,
    89, 90, 91, 92, 93, 95, 129, 133, 134, 188
Christian V, King, 62, 63
Christiansø, 62, 63, 162, 163, 176, 177
Christo, Convento de, 14
Chronicles, 96
Cistercians, 16, 17, 29, 30, 33, 35, 36, 39,
    133, 135, 136, 183, 184
Citeaux, 17, 29, 30, 183
Clairvaux, 16, 17, 28, 29, 32 - 36, 38, 39, 78,
    87, 130, 133, 135, 183, 185

Clement, Saint, 59, 119
Clement V, Pope, 184
Cleophas, 91
Clermont, 23, 183
Colombier, Pierre de, 17
Constantine, 24, 27, 87, 88, 93, 94, 183, 189
Conte du Graal, Le, 78
Copenhagen, 45, 62, 185
Cornford, Prof. Christopher, 64, 119
Corvus, 44, 187, 188
Crater, 188
Cromlech, 70, 72
Cubit, 105, 106, 109, 111 - 114, 138

D'Arcons, César, 136
Dagobert, King, 11, 183
Dargun, 33
Dead Sea Scrolls, 28, 99
Denmark, 3, 4, 14, 15, 30 - 35, 39, 45, 62,
    183, 185
Descartes, René, 126
Dijon, 11, 29
Disme, La, 74
Dome of the Rock, 96
Dover, 20
Dunkirk, 73

Egypt, 19, 45, 109, 111 - 113, 138, 188
Eldena, 33
Elias, 92
Eskil, 32 - 36, 87, 130, 133, 135, 136, 183
Esrom, 33
Essenes, 134
Estonia, 35, 36, 38, 39, 135, 183, 184
Euclid, 20
Eudes I, Duke of Burgundy, 29
Eunate, 20
Evreux, 187, 188
Ezekiel, Book of, 98, 99

Fibonacci series, 65
Flinders Petrie, William Matthew, 109, 110, 185
Fontaines, 29
Fontevrault, 20
Foot, 73, 74, 80, 82, 106
Försvunden Teknik, 102, 185
Freemasonry, 25 - 27, 73, 80, 82, 87, 92, 94,
    95,106, 133, 134, 188, 189
Fulcanelli, 17, 18, 185
Fulco, 35, 39, 183

Galileo, 83, 124, 130
Gardner, Laurence, 24, 91, 185
Germany, 15, 31, 32, 136

Gihon, Spring of, 28, 29, 96 - 99, 104, 106
Gilbert, Adrian, 187
Gill, Dan, 104, 185
Giza, 187
Gizabethe, 114, 138
Glastonbury, 91
Golden Fleece, Order of the, 11, 17
Golden Section, 64 - 66, 70, 119 - 122, 158,
    164, 173
Gorm, King, 30
Gothic, 15 - 18, 20, 57, 58, 78, 132, 135, 186
Gothland, 35, 39, 135
Grammaticus, Saxo, 10, 185
Gudhjem, 63
Gustav III, King, 95
Gustav VI Adolf, King, 95

Hamburg, 31, 34
Hanseatic League, 35
Hastings, Battle of, 30
Hebrew University, 100, 101, 104, 185
Helena, 24, 25, 27, 28, 87 - 89, 93, 94, 183
Henry I, King, 72
Henry II, King, 34
Herrevad, 33
Hezekiah, 96, 97, 100, 101, 104 - 106, 109, 183
Holland, 11, 74
Holy Blood & the Holy Grail, The, 5, 27, 78,
    133, 185
Holy Grail, 77, 78, 79, 106, 135, 136, 188
Holy Place, The, 5, 28, 45, 47, 64, 69, 72,
    80, 185
Holy Roman Emperor, see Barbarossa,
    Frederick
Holy Sepulchre, Church of the, 23 - 25, 36, 88,
    89, 92, 94, 95, 133, 134, 183, 189
Høybygde, 63
Hvide (White) family, 31, 32
Hydra, 188, 189

Inch, 19, 73 -75, 80, 81, 109, 110, 120
Institut Géographique, 47
Islam, 23, 133

James, Saint, 59, 61, 91 - 93, 125
Jason, 17
Jebusites, 96, 97
Jerusalem, 14, 16, 23, 24, 27 - 30, 34, 36, 79,
    89, 91, 92, 94 - 96, 99 - 102, 104 - 106,
    133, 134, 136, 183, 184
JMPFW Ltd, 95
Joab, 96
Joachim, 89

John, Saint, 90 - 93
Judah, Tribe of, 99
Judicature des Allemands, 136
Jura, mountains, 11
Juvelius, Dr. Valter Henrik, 28, 98, 99, 102, 103, 133, 184

Key to the Sacred Pattern, The, 5, 69, 74, 129, 185
Kidron valley, 106
Kirkholmen, see Christiansø
Kjellson, Henry, 102, 103, 185
Klemensker, 54, 58, 59, 64, 118, 119, 123, 161 - 163, 169 - 171, 177
Knud, King, 12, 13, 30
Knudsker, 66, 115, 116, 118 - 122, 124, 172, 174, 177, 179 - 181
Knytlinge Saga, 12, 13, 14, 185
Kolbatz, 33
Kolchis, 17
Kort & Matrikelstyrelsen, 47, 54, 153
Kotjanski, A.A., 121

La Celle, 35
Laon, 20
Latvia, 35
Lavard, Knud, 31, 35, 36
Le Puy, 20
League, Domesday, 73, 74
Leigh, Richard, 5
Lind, Prof. Niels, 143, 144
Liste, 63
Lithuania, 35
Livonia, see Sword, Brothers of the
London, 20
Long-Haired Kings, 10
Lorraine, 133
Lost Treasure of Jerusalem...? The, 5
Lund, 31 - 36, 39

Mark, Saint, 90, 92
Matthew, Saint, 90
Merovingian, 10, 11, 133, 134, 183
Messianic Legacy, The, 5, 100, 185
Metz, 20
Midgaardsormen, 189
Mile, 69, 70, 72 - 76, 80, 106, 109, 112, 120, 127, 138
Mile, Statute, 74, 80, 138
Millén, Johan, 28, 29, 95 - 103, 106, 133, 134, 184, 185
Mogstad, Sverre Dag, 26, 27, 93, 95, 185, 189
Molay, Jacques de, 26, 94, 184
Montbard, André de, 30, 134

Montmajour, 20
Montmorillon, 20
Moses, 92, 93, 183
Muslim, 19, 23, 24

Napoleon, 134
NASA, 80, 83
Nebuchadnezzar, 99, 100, 183
Neussere, Pharaoh, 111
Nicodemus, 90 - 93
Nielsen, Finn Ole Sonne, 55
Nørlund, Prof. P.E., 45, 185
North Pole, 72, 81, 82, 109, 111, 112,
Northampton, 20
Norway, 13, 30, 33
Notre Dame, 16, 188
Nydalal, 33
Nyker, 48, 55, 60, 115, 143, 148, 152, 156 - 160, 162, 164, 166, 177, 179 - 181
Nylars, 37, 48, 50 - 52, 58 - 60, 64, 66, 76, 115, 117, 118, 120, 121, 123, 132, 143, 145, 152, 154, 155, 158, 160 - 165, 177, 178

Odin, 12, 13
Øland, 36, 39
Olivia, 33
Olsker, 48, 51, 55, 60, 61, 115, 137, 138, 143, 146, 147, 150 - 152, 155 - 160, 162, 164, 166, 177 - 181
Ophel, Mount, 134
Orion Mystery, The, 187
Orosius, 11
Øsel, 36
Osiris, 187, 188
Østerlars, 21, 22, 43, 48 - 52, 58 - 60, 64, 66, 76, 115 - 118, 120, 121, 123 - 125, 131, 137, 143, 145, 152 - 156, 158, 160 - 164, 166, 168, 177, 178
Østermarie, 143
Ouroboros, 189

På Rätta Vägar, 98, 102
Palestine, 14, 23, 28, 94
Paris, 20, 112, 184
Parker Expedition, 95, 98, 101, 133
Paschal III, anti-pope, 35
Paulsen, Hubert, 111, 185
Payens, Hugues de, 28, 30, 94
Pedersker, 143
Pentagonal figures, 64 - 67, 69, 70, 81, 115, 116, 118, 119, 123, 124, 131, 164, 165, 178
Perceval, 106
Pharisees, 91

Pi, 19, 75, 76, 80, 106, 110 - 112, 114, 116, 117, 120, 121, 172, 173, 185
Pilate, 90
Pole measure, 72 - 75, 80 - 82, 109, 112
Portugal, 14, 20
Poussin, Nicolas, 64
Povlsker, 124, 125, 173, 174, 177, 179, 180, 181
Priest, the Painter & the Devil, The, 5
Pyramid, 19, 45, 87, 109 - 114, 187
Pyrenees, 3, 5
Pythagoras, 20, 65

Qumran, 134

Ragnarsen, Eigil, 12, 13, 14
Reims, 187, 188
Rennes-le-Château, 5, 11, 47, 64, 69, 70, 72, 74, 88, 105, 129 - 131, 133, 136, 137, 143, 184
Rhine, River, 11
Riga, 39, 135, 184
Rø, 54, 62, 64, 163, 164, 177, 178
Roma, 35, 39, 135
Roskilde, 31, 32, 36
Rügen, 15, 32
Russia, 35
Rutsker, 50, 58, 118, 119, 123, 168 - 171 177 - 179

Saaremaa, 36
Salisbury, 35
Samuel, 96
Sang Raal, 78
Sanhedrin, 91, 95
Saunière, Bérenger, 5, 11, 70, 87, 129, 132, 138, 184
Scandinavia, 9, 10, 14, 26, 30, 33, 35, 95
Schonfield, Dr. Hugh, 79, 99, 133, 186
Scotland, 30
Secret, The, 5
Sède, Gérard de, 5
Segovia, 20
Seshat, 111
Shadow of the Templars, The, 5
Siloam, Pool of, 28, 98, 99, 104
Simon, son of Cleophas, 91
Sion, Mount, 133, 135, 183
Sion, Prieuré de, 138
Solomon, King, 16, 28, 96, 122, 134, 135, 183
Sophia, see Baphomet
Sorø, 33

Spain, 20, 73
Stables of Solomon, 28, 94, 135
Starck, J.A., 92 - 94, 133
Stevin, Simon, 74
Stockholm, 98
Stromata, 59
Svanicke, 63
Sven, 31, 32
Sweden, 26, 30, 62, 95
Sword, Brothers of the, 33, 39, 184

Templar, Knights, 14, 16, 17, 20, 22, 25 - 36, 39, 43, 72, 77 - 79, 87, 92 - 95, 99, 105, 106, 113, 124, 130, 133 - 137, 183, 184, 188, 189
Thiende, La, 74
Thor, 12, 13
Tomar, 14, 20
Torres del Rio, 20
Transfiguration, the, 91 - 93
Treiden, Theoderik von, 39, 184
Trelleborg, 45, 46
Troyes, 30, 39, 78, 183
Troyes, Chrétien de, 78

Urban II, Pope, 23, 183
Ursa Major, 188

Valdemar the Great, King, 15, 31, 32, 34 - 36, 183
Vestermarie, 52 - 54, 59, 160, 161, 177, 178
Victor IV, anti-pope, 34, 35
Vincent, Dr. Henri, 100, 101, 186
Virgin Mary, 89, 90, 188
Virgo, 89, 187
Vitskøl, 33
Vraie Langue Celtique, la, 70, 75, 185

Weimar, 92
Wends, 15, 32
Winchester, 30
Wisdom, Father of, 95, 133
Wivel, Mette, 14, 22
Wolfsen, Herman Bohn, 62, 63
Wood, David, 69
Wulfstan, 10

Zadoch, Sons of, 134
Zeruiah, 96
Zion, Mount, 96, 97, 99
Zuckerman, A.J., 27, 186